How To Home School

A Practical Approach

PARENT-TEACHER COLLECTION

by Gayle Graham

Common Sense Press
™

Cover photo: © Comstock, Inc. 1997

© *Copyright 1992, Gayle Graham*
Common Sense Press • P.O. Box 1365
8786 Highway 21 • Melrose, FL 32666
ISBN 1-880892-40-5

ACKNOWLEDGEMENTS

For over ten years, I've taught "How to Home School" seminars and privately consulted beginning homeschool parents. In each session, without exception, I've learned something new. *Each of you has insight into how your children learn best and what works!* Thanks to all of you who've sharpened my homeschooling skills.

We learn to teach well by modelling good teachers. For me, Jessica Hulcy and Carole Thaxton (authors of Konos Character Curriculum) have served as role models. Thank you Jessica and Carole, for personally encouraging me and so many others to ignite a fervent love of learning in our children.

I love sharing what I've learned with others, but without the non-stop encouragement of my husband, Lee, this book would have never *even been started. I laughed out loud at the very idea, but he kept repeating, "I really think you should write a book!"* Thank you Lee, for your confidence, persistence, and prayer.

Those prayers were answered when an editor, Ken Emery, happened into one of our seminars. "Gayle," he said, "it would be a simple matter to turn your seminar notes into a book." To think I actually believed him! It turned out that Ken's idea of simple and mine *were two entirely different things.* Thank you so much Ken, for your practical skills which enabled me to capture these ideas on paper in readable form.

Finally, I remember our five beautiful daughters. Each of you has *been used by God to teach me how children really learn.* Thank you for being my guinea pigs, and for your longsuffering. You've shared your Mom with other homeschoolers, sometimes for days.

Over the years as I've compiled seminar notes and written outlines, I've continually said, "If this is just for my grandchildren, it will be worth it!" This book is dedicated to my daughters — our next generation's home teachers.

Table of Contents

Section One — Foundations for Excellence

Chapter 1— *Why Home School?* 3

    Individual Learning Differences 8

    Academic, Social & Emotional Benefits 6-10

    The Last WORD 12

Chapter 2— *Planning for Success* 15

    Organization 21

        Taking Control of Household Chores 22

        Management Tools for Home and School 26

        Home Management Notebook 27

        School Management Notebook 27

        Child's Notebook 27

    Planning and Goals 42

    Covering All the Bases 45

Section Two — Language Arts

Chapter 1— *Reading—De-mystified* 53

    Readiness 55

    Beginning Reading 60

    Rapid Development of Skills 73

    Wide Reading 77

        Comprehension Skills 77

        Vocabulary 82

    Refinement of Reading 85

Chapter 2— **Taking the Worry out of Writing** 89

    Why Do We Write? / What Should We Write About? 91

    Developing and Coaching Young Writers 97

        Easing into Writing 103

        What's A Mother to Do? 106

    Mastering the Mechanics 110

        Spelling 111

        Handwriting 113

        Grammar 114

Section Three — Pulling It All Together

Chapter 1— *Learning and Exploring Together* *121*

Unit Studies— Take Your Time 123

BIRD BINGE 124

Real-life Learning 125

DOUBTING DADS — "WHAT ABOUT STANDARDIZED TESTING?" ... 126

Unit Study Advantages 129

WHAT TO INCLUDE IN A UNIT STUDY 132

Assessing Unit Study Curriculum Choices 134

Record-keeping 134

What About Social Studies and Science? 135

WHAT'S INCLUDED IN SOCIAL STUDIES 136

WHAT'S INCLUDED IN SCIENCE 138

Chapter 2— *Math —The Home School Advantage* *143*

Math Readiness 146

Elementary Math 149

Computation 149

Place Values *149*

Fractions *149*

Time *151*

Money *151*

Problem Solving 152

Final Thoughts 154

APPENDIX A. .... *Choosing Curriculum*

APPENDIX B. .... *Understanding Standardized Testing*

APPENDIX C. .... *Reproducible Forms*

HOUSEKEEPING

CURRICULUM SCOPE

SCHEDULE WEEK AT A GLANCE

COORDINATING A NUMBER OF CHILDREN

WEEKLY ASSIGNMENT SHEET

UNIT STUDY PLANS

PROGRAM OF STUDY

REGISTRY OF GREAT READING

YEARLY GOALS

MONTHLY GOALS

Preface—
A Glimpse at the Grahams

[**Note from the Editor:** This manual on homeschooling is borne out of the practical experience of a *veteran homeschool Mom*. (Gayle also has all the right educational credentials as well, though she says she has overcome that problem!) Before plunging into all the "how-to" content of this book, perhaps you would enjoy this brief glimpse into the Graham household *(excerpted from the article "Terrific Toddlers" by Kathy von Duyke, **KONOS Helps**, January 1991.)*]

Picture two-year-old Meg standing in the toilet— during school hours. At two-and-a half, she took her mom over to [a] timeline because she had found Beethoven by herself. This same child went to the art museum, curled up under the elbow of a tour guide holding a painting and said, *"Oh! That's **The Dancer** by Renoir."* At three she cut her hair to look like a Massai warrior. You might ask, *"What preschool could ever offer this child a richer environment?"* Then again, *"Can this child be salvaged?"*

Gayle Graham is Meg's mother, and she and her husband, Lee, have been homeschooling for nine years. Their other daughters are: Ashley (15), Amy (12), Heather (8), and Britt (2). Gayle says, *"I never realized how much a toddler could learn. I'm not a pushy mom, but I'm amazed at what a young child is interested in — they don't need watered down stuff."*

Lee is a stockbroker and certified financial planner and Gayle's biggest cheerleader. (He thinks homeschooling is the greatest and tells everyone so.) Gayle is a wife, mother, and educational consultant.

She was a public school teacher who taught 4th and 5th grade for six years, but she retired when her first child was born. Later she was approached by Dr. Robin Barton (who operates an educational counseling center) to consult with a local school on a part-time basis. *"I said I could only work two hours per day when my babies were napping (a Christian friend across the street stayed with my babies) and she said, 'fine.' "* says Gayle. Under Dr. Barton's tutelage, she did psychoeducational testing, tutoring, and observed students in the classroom in order to make recommendations for teachers. She soon found she needed more background for the job and started evening graduate school.

By the time she had finished graduate school Gayle says, *"I was sick of the educational pride in the university and wanted nothing more to do with education."* She and her family went into short term missions for seven months. She told no one of her educational experience, wanting instead to be involved in mercy ministries. (There were a lot of refugees pouring out of Cambodia at the time). *"After a few months of intensive training,"* says Gayle, *"our leaders approached us and said that God had spoken to their hearts about me and wanted me to establish a mini-school for the children of the parents on our team. I felt like Jonah who had been discovered and wanted no part of the plan!"*

Lee and God convinced her to do it, and this became her first "homeschooling" experience. The parents were highly involved in their children's studies, and the children were in school only in the morning hours. Then they ministered alongside their parents in the afternoon and evening. *"My duties were to develop curriculum, learning centers, and activities and to supervise selected tutors for the children."*

After returning home, Lee and Gayle worked for 18 months to try to establish a good Christian school in their city. Through studying the Bible and talking to many Christian educators, they formed a philosophy of education. Plans for the school, however, fell through two weeks before the doors were to open. Public school or a Christian school that used cubicles and workbooks were not an option. Lee and Ashley asked Gayle to teach at home. *"The idea was unthinkable to me! I had never read a book about homeschooling, nor had I even heard the term."*

After prayer Gayle felt that this was indeed what God would have her do. The only curriculum she knew of was a workbook/textbook approach that was "a real killer". Ashley and she learned that if they worked really fast through the workbooks, they could get to the fun stuff — hands-on in the kitchen. *"After one semester of this, I again did the unthinkable! I threw away the workbooks and started developing my own units. I had witnessed for myself what turned Ashley on to learning and I could see where the most education was really taking place."*

"At the end of the following year, I went to our state's first homeschool bookfair. I saw for myself others who were doing exactly what I had been attempting to do. They even had the same goals — Christlike character for their children and a hands-on approach to unit studies. I was hooked!"

Meanwhile Gayle's educational consulting was taking a homeschooling bent. People started coming to her for help. She started an educational testing business, began doing *How to Homeschool* seminars, and did a lot of curriculum planning with individuals.

The Grahams put their principles into practice at home. Their schoolroom is in a small den-sized room off the kitchen, outfitted over the years with a table, blackboard and bookshelves. A gate across the doorway allows Gayle to go in to instruct for short periods while Meg and Britt play in sight in the kitchen. While the older girls are doing paperwork, Gayle can be with Britt and Meg, but still be available for help. She uses several gates throughout the house to keep the toddlers from trashing rooms while Gayle is teaching.

Mom uses breakfast as a time to pray with the children for the day, read a portion of scripture, or discuss what they were meditating on during their quiet time. Breakfast is followed by chores.

The older children then begin individual study while Gayle spends time with the toddlers. She starts teaching most mornings about quarter 'til ten. *"This is a low key time"*, says Gayle,*"We do lots of reading and I'm real big on vocabulary. If you know the vocabulary, you know the subject..it's vital."* They do simple activities, and Gayle includes Meg and Britt in this time by reading to them as well. (No, Meg and Britt are not always good, nor do they always sit still.) When she comes across a good passage for it, Gayle will paraphrase something that the girls all dramatize, getting them all involved. For instance while reading that the Massai made houses out of cow dung, the girls quickly pretended to do this with old blankets, etc. Now Meg delights in telling unprepared adults, *"Did you know Massai warriors build their houses with cow dung?"*

Gayle doesn't require the toddlers to stay and they mostly follow their own interests. She's always prepared however, with something to include them. When they were studying atomic research, the older girls were doing chemistry projects in the kitchen. Britt, then 16 months, was given a salt and pepper shaker so she could experiment, too. When studying electricity, Meg (at age two) also received a set of batteries, bulbs, and wires. She figured out how to get hers to light by experimenting and watching the others.

Because a teaching timeline is posted at eye level opposite the breakfast and lunch counter, the girls are always looking at it. Casual conversation about the timeline has enabled Meg to learn nearly every figure by name. [Perhaps] Meg figured out the Beethoven character because the timeline figure's crazy hairdo was like the picture on the tape they listened to.

Gayle also enlists the help of Lee and grandparents. [Occasionally] she invites the grandparents over for Sunday afternoon supper. While she cooks, the children pair up with a grandparent or dad and walk through centers Gayle has set up around the

The Grahams put their principles into practice at home. Their schoolroom is in a small den-sized room off the kitchen, outfitted over the years with a table, blackboard and bookshelves. A gate across the doorway allows Gayle to go in to instruct for short periods while Meg and Britt play in sight in the kitchen. While the older girls are doing paperwork, Gayle can be with Britt and Meg, but still be available for help. She uses several gates throughout the house to keep the toddlers from trashing rooms while Gayle is teaching.

Mom uses breakfast as a time to pray with the children for the day, read a portion of scripture, or discuss what they were meditating on during their quiet time. Breakfast is followed by chores.

The older children then begin individual study while Gayle spends time with the toddlers. She starts teaching most mornings about quarter 'til ten. *"This is a low key time"*, says Gayle,*"We do lots of reading and I'm real big on vocabulary. If you know the vocabulary, you know the subject..it's vital."* They do simple activities, and Gayle includes Meg and Britt in this time by reading to them as well. (No, Meg and Britt are not always good, nor do they always sit still.) When she comes across a good passage for it, Gayle will paraphrase something that the girls all dramatize, getting them all involved. For instance while reading that the Massai made houses out of cow dung, the girls quickly pretended to do this with old blankets, etc. Now Meg delights in telling unprepared adults, *"Did you know Massai warriors build their houses with cow dung?"*

Gayle doesn't require the toddlers to stay and they mostly follow their own interests. She's always prepared however, with something to include them. When they were studying atomic research, the older girls were doing chemistry projects in the kitchen. Britt, then 16 months, was given a salt and pepper shaker so she could experiment, too. When studying electricity, Meg (at age two) also received a set of batteries, bulbs, and wires. She figured out how to get hers to light by experimenting and watching the others.

Because a teaching timeline is posted at eye level opposite the breakfast and lunch counter, the girls are always looking at it. Casual conversation about the timeline has enabled Meg to learn nearly every figure by name. [Perhaps] Meg figured out the Beethoven character because the timeline figure's crazy hairdo was like the picture on the tape they listened to.

Gayle also enlists the help of Lee and grandparents. [Occasionally] she invites the grandparents over for Sunday afternoon supper. While she cooks, the children pair up with a grandparent or dad and walk through centers Gayle has set up around the house. For instance, while studying birds, they might stop at a table and go through reference books looking for birds with different beaks and feet, then try to guess what they eat. At the next stop, they might make a bird feeder, and at another stop listen to bird calls and try to identify them. The grandparents think it's great because they get to see what the kids are learning. Their skepticism about homeschooling has changed to a favorable impression, especially after seeing what the toddlers know.

The Grahams believe Godly character is even more important than academics. (Gayle will take time out from teaching to deal with discipline if necessary.) There is a real balance of discipline and love apparent in their home. House rules include no crying or tantrums — though the two youngest are still learning the rules. Her girls memorize scripture which addresses specific flaws or needs. Gayle also posts scriptures around the house. *"You become what you meditate upon"* says Gayle. One of her favorites is *"All your 'daughters' will be taught by the Lord, and great will be your children's peace."*

Meg's Toddler Tip

My Mom bought both me and Britt a plastic, postcard-sized frame to put in our room. Then she took us to the art museum and we selected lots of postcard sized reprints of artwork. She said they were cheap, so she let us get a whole bag full. Now we get to choose which print we want in our room. We look at it for a few weeks, talk about it, use it with our dolls, learn the name of the work and the artist. Mom says if we look at one print each day for four weeks and then review that print once a month for a year, we will never forget it. Then, when we're eighteen we can take a CLEP test (whatever that is) and get college credit for fine arts courses without ever having to sit through a class!

THIS IS A WORKING MANUAL!

THERE ARE MARGINS AND EXTRA PAGES
THROUGHOUT FOR TAKING NOTES.
(YOU CAN EVEN ADD YOUR OWN
GOOD IDEAS.)

MAKE IT YOUR PERSONAL HANDBOOK
FOR HOMESCHOOL SUCCESS!

In this section...

- *Why ask why?*

- *The nuts and bolts—planning and organizing for success*

Section One
Foundations for Excellence

"My utmost goal is to teach you to teach your children." —*Gayle Graham*

If you're like most folks who've decided to homeschool, you face a lot of mixed emotions— from enthusiasm to a slight twinge of apprehension.

Maybe you're a little confused with all the choices in curriculum and instruction. Recordkeeping seems overwhelming. What if you overlook something? Or, maybe you're just not quite sure about how to pull your program together. Well, whether you're a seasoned homeschooler or a novice, this manual is for *you*.

Homeschooling began for the Graham family in 1982. Ever since, I've had a desire to set a foundation for excellence in our home-school and help you do the same in yours. My purpose is not to convince you to homeschool (there are lots of fine books already on that topic), but to give you the nuts and bolts of *how* to homeschool — a practical, working guide for your homeschool. My utmost goal is to teach you to teach your children.

If God has called you to home school, He wants you to excel in what He has called you to do! I hope this book helps you to be an excellent home educator. (And please let me know how it has helped you or any suggestions you have for improvement. My publisher's address is in the front of this book!)

May God bless you and your family as you do exactly what He has called you to do in educating your children at home.

In this chapter...

- ## Why ask why?

- ## Learning Differences

- ## Homeschool Benefits

Section One, Chapter One
Why Home School?

"And all your children shall be disciples, taught of the Lord and obedient to His will, and great shall be the peace of your children."
                                                    —Isaiah 54:13

"**W**hy are you homeschooling?" If you haven't been asked that question yet, you soon will. But even if no one else ever asks, it's absolutely necessary to ask yourself— and wait for a clear answer.

You are probably anxious to dig into teacher's manuals, start planning your lessons and get going on all the practical elements of homeschooling, but before you do that it is really vital for your survival to consider exactly why you are homeschooling.

Know your reasons. Know if indeed God is asking you to do this for your children. Because if you don't know for sure that He has led you to homeschool, when things get a little tough it might be hard for you to stick with it! And I can assure you that in February, when it has been raining for 21 days straight (as it did in our state one year) it feels a little tough at times.

There are many valid answers to our question. Let's look at a few.

Builds Godly Character
Most of you tell me that character training is the most important element of your home school. You want your children to have Godly character traits: attentiveness, flexibility, joyfulness, obedience, responsibility, organizational habits, creativity. The list of Godly character traits that we want to impart to our children is endless. Instead of saying that a trained, knowledgeable mind will conquer bad habits, we say Godly character will place a person in a position where he can be trained to do something positive with the knowledge he acquires!

We all know educated fools. I'm talking about adults who are extremely well educated, but in fact don't know how to properly use their knowledge.

A *Wall Street Journal* interviewer asked businesses the question, *"What do you most desire of college graduates?"* The answer was that businesses desire men and women who are honest, diligent, and who work hard. These are all character qualities!

Homeschoolers have four advantages in developing character.

First of all, the best part of the child's day is right at home with the parent. You have those daily golden opportunities to instill values in your child. If you are with your own children most of the day, you won't miss those quality times.

A myth circulating in our society says we don't need quantity time with our children, we need quality time. But if you think about it, you know as well as I do that no one can plan golden moments. You *can't* plan them. They just happen. If you're not there for that golden opportunity to instill a value in your child, it's gone!

Homeschooled children develop character in the home through modelling. As the old adage goes *"Values are caught, not taught."* The most productive way to teach our children our values is not sitting with them at the end of the evening, reading them a Bible story (although this is a good habit to form.) The best way to help our children develop Godly character is through modelling it ourselves. The more time they spend with us, the more they will see that role model.

I don't have to tell you what peer role models do to our children. We do not want our children to learn their values from other children. We want them to learn character and Godly values from us. The more time they spend with us, the more opportunity they will have to learn our character traits.

Homeschool youngsters develop character through work involvement. A few years ago, there was an article entitled **Success Secret** (based on George & Caroline Vaillant's report in the American Journal of Psychiatry.) Researchers from Harvard University did a long-term study of how success in adulthood related to what had happened in the same adults' childhood.

They studied 456 men from childhood until age 47. The researchers discovered that those who had worked hardest as children developed into the best paid and most satisfied family men.

Their work as youngsters had usually consisted of household chores, part-time jobs, sports, and studies. The least hardworking children in this group later encountered the most unemployment and unhappiness, as well as a higher death rate.

We have natural opportunities in our home for our children to work around the house or yard, or in a business.

I can tell you story after story of homeschooled boys and girls who have started their own businesses. Ryan, a little boy here in our town, had a baking business at the age of eight. He earned well over $100 profit per month baking and delivering coffee cakes once a week to local nursing homes. There are other examples of homeschooled children who start businesses or help their parents in already existing businesses.

Our children need to be exposed to the adult world of work. The teen years are an ideal time for apprenticeship experiences with a parent or other appropriate model. Children benefit from working whether or not that job leads to a lifetime career.

Finally, our children develop character through service. When we prepare a pot of soup for the neighbor down the street who has been ill and we let our children help us, we are teaching our children to serve those who are in need.

Work and service are two keys to combat the prevailing egocentricism in our society. A lie circulating in our society is that we need to fulfill ourselves — to be free to attain our highest potential. This is simply not true. Why are we here? We are here to be the best we can be to the glory of God and to serve others. We are not here for ourselves.

So, you are homeschooling because God has called you to this task and because of your priorities— especially character development. But if you are aware of even more benefits, you will have more enthusiasm and stamina for the long haul. (By the way, let your children know the benefits of home education. Let them know what they are receiving so that they'll appreciate it, too.)

Academic Benefits

There are 100 or more individual daily adult responses between the parent and the child in the home school environment. (Don't ask me who sat down and counted them, but researchers who have observed and counted daily adult responses between parent and child came up with 100 or more daily.) Just for comparison, how many responses do you think they found between teacher and child in the average classroom? The answer? Between 0-6.

Your homeschool can be totally individualized.
You can have a program that is totally geared to each child's specific interests and needs. This just isn't feasible in a typical classroom situation where a curriculum must be followed for a group of children. In the homeschool, you have the privilege of skipping spelling words if your child already knows them or skipping phonics lessons if they do not apply to your child. You have the freedom to move a child ahead in math or hold him back for a few extra days until a needed skill is mastered. (Homeschool parents can also take advantage of each child's unique abilities—see **Individual Learning Differences**, pages 8-9.) Only home-schoolers can optimize the program of study for each student.

2 hours = 6
Research has also shown that *two hours of homeschool is equivalent to six hours of classroom instruction.* That means your little one has four extra hours in the school day for work, service projects, or just plain thinking.

Real-life experience vs. theory
You have the chance to have less seatwork in your home school and more chance for learning via projects, hands-on, discovery, experiments, and field trips.

You don't have to keep a classroom of children busy while you are working with a reading group. Your children do only as much paperwork as is necessary to master content.

Student-centered

You also have the possibility for a less didactic learning environment. By that, I mean, less teacher-centered, more student-centered. Typically, we're used to seeing a classroom teacher stand in front of a group and present the lesson. The teacher has the information and she imparts it to the child.

In the home, however, we have the opportunity to not only impart information, but also interact with and lead our children into ways of finding information on their own. They become far more involved in the learning process. (I, for one, am glad that I don't need to be an expert in every subject area in order to be able to do this!)

Pulling it all together as a family

Finally, you have the possibility for interrelating units of study—learning and exploring together as a family.

For example when you study the Revolutionary War, you might study heat because of the firearms that were used (science), or make tin lanterns (art) or take a trip to the silversmith's shop.

The possibilities for exploring interrelating subject areas are endless when you use the unit approach. (We'll take an in-depth look at this approach in Section Three.)

Of course, if you use the unit approach, you won't teach the way you were taught in school. You won't be standing in front of the child imparting information or having a child read a chapter, answer questions, and regurgitate information for a test. It will be a totally different and exciting way of teaching. And the great news is that research has shown this is how children learn best.

INDIVIDUAL LEARNING DIFFERENCES

We humans are all unique. Stop and think about it. Each person is a unique blend of strengths, weaknesses, gifts, talents, and skills. It can get downright confusing.

Our tendency as humans is to try to peg our children. Peg their learning style, and we will know what to do with them. That gives us comfort. But, guess what? God is greater than that. He doesn't duplicate people. Each is different from the next.

It does help us though, to try to see patterns in our children. Understanding each child's natural strengths and weaknesses helps us to know better who they are and how to cooperate with God in His calling upon their lives.

Two Basic Bodystyles

What are some differences to look for? The most obvious is male/female. Generally, but not always, boys are risktakers. They question your choices and like a challenge. Challenges to them may or may not involve the physical. Boys are open and honest, too. Girls are more inclined to be pleasers, helpers, peacemakers. They are created to be helpmeets. They need your approval. Yet girls are persuasive, designed to influence others.

Perceptual Strengths/Weaknesses

Learning tasks, whether they be reading, math, or writing, require three senses: visual, auditory, or kinesthetic/tactile. Children who prefer to learn visually are generally early readers and good spellers. They also don't balk at workbooks. (Our schools were designed for visually strong learners.) Auditory learners obviously like audio tapes, talking to friends, and music. Kinesthetic learners like to move, dance, run. But don't expect them to be early readers or spellers.

A visual child may produce a chart. An auditory child will enjoy producing a play. A kinesthetic child will teach the younger children a skill with a moving game he creates. Projects and hands-on make learning come alive for all children.

Much has been written about pinpointing children's learning styles, but beware! There are more factors to consider than just perceptual! All young children (under 5-7 years old) have kinesthetic needs. They have short attention spans and need to move when they learn. Intermediate children have great memories. Their learning curve jumps overnight. Older students are more critical. (Ask any mother of a 12 year old.) Their critical thinking skills are developing, but they are more argumentative, too.

There is also some danger in pegging a person too quickly. For example, all five of my children love hands-on projects but not all five of them are kinesthetic learners. We all learn well by doing. On the other hand, one child's perceptual weakness is visual. Therefore I will teach new material to her strength — kinesthetic, but I will also try to train her weak visual area with practice. Use the strength, develop the weakness.

Use the child's strengths to teach a new or difficult area. Success breeds success. But incorporate all learning modalities (auditory, visual, kinesthetic) in teaching. Develop weak areas. We should strive to help each child become well-rounded.

Left-brain, Right-brain? — Why waste half a brain??

Some children rely more on the right side of their brains and others on the left side of their brains. Typically, right-brained people are artistic, sensitive, and non-verbal. Left-brained folks are more logical and verbal. But guess what? God gave us whole brains! We are to develop weak areas and use our strengths. Why waste half a brain?

Personality/Temperament

Psychologists tell us there are four basic temperaments, but no one has to tell that to the parents of more than one child. We know that each is stamped with his own distinct personality from birth. One baby comes out demanding room service every two hours, or else! Another is amiable and peaceful, content to smile at passers-by. We certainly didn't do anything to make them different. Each child comes equipped with his or her own basic personality.

As we mature, though, we are to become more Christ-like, utilizing our God-given strengths, rising above our human weaknesses. So, we may need to encourage one child not to be so bossy and to control his temper (while rejoicing in his leadership capabilities) and counsel another about God's perspective on moodiness (while rejoicing in his empathy with those who are suffering). Develop strengths. Overcome weaknesses.

Birth Order

We haven't even mentioned birth order. Your first child, simply because he is first, has plenty of opportunity for fellowship with adults. He enjoys adult conversation, and feels comfortable with older folks. If there are younger children in the family, he learns to be a caretaker too. The last child usually loves to have a crowd around, preferably an audience. He's always laughing and being cute. A middle child has another set of challenges, etc.

Of course, each child's birth order is out of our control completely. Yet, God doesn't make mistakes. Birth order is part of God's plan and preparation for your child's life.

God's Design, God's Calling, God's Plan

How do we make sense of all these learning and personality patterns? We must look prayerfully at the big picture. Strengths and tendencies emerge as your child grows.

What has God called him to be? Perhaps your strong visual son who loves to read and is a critical, even argumentative thinker is destined to be a lawyer or lobbyist who will make a difference. Or, your sensitive, kinesthetic daughter who loves animals but doesn't mind getting dirty outside playing soccer, will someday be on the mission field, living without what we consider the necessities of life. Or, that auditory, sanguine daughter who loves to talk and be with friends will become president of the women of the church. What an exciting opportunity we have as parents to cooperate with God as He prepares an individual for life's calling!

Social & Emotional Benefits

What bothers parents <u>most</u> about public schools? Textbooks? Poor teachers? Sex education? If I surveyed you, I'll bet you'd say the greatest threat to our children in the schools is *peer pressure*. I don't need to tell you what peer pressure does to our children.

In his tape series, **Preparing for Adolescence**, Christian psychologist, Dr. James Dobson relates a true account of a research project. Several groups were chosen and one group was taken at a time to study what the responses of the individuals would be.

The researchers told each group they were going to ask some simple questions that would require simple answers. One person, who did not know it, was the "dummy" of the group. In other words, the dummy was the person who did not know the trick.

Three lines were drawn on the blackboard. One of the lines was obviously shorter than the others. The question was asked, *"Which is the shortest of the three lines?"* The respondents were simply to raise their hand when the person who was leading this investigation pointed to the shortest line.

The researcher's focus was the behavior of the dummy in the group. Everyone else had been told to raise their hands for the *second* shortest line instead of the shortest line in order to fool the dummy.

Each time the instructor pointed to the shortest line. The dummy quickly raised his hand. He looked around and saw he was the only one with his hand raised. When the instructor pointed to the second shortest line, the rest of the group raised their hands.

The researchers repeated this experiment with several groups and observed that after a few trials, invariably the dummy began to raise his hand with the group. Experiments with groups of all ages— adults, youths, teenagers proved the same results. Whether the dummy was an adult or teenager, he almost always changed his mind to go along with the group (75% of the sample).

Peer pressure is powerful. Even the adults in the experiment could not stand the pressure. They raised their hands for a line which they knew was an incorrect response to a question that had an obvious answer.

Peer groups don't teach social skills. They teach us to conform— to want to be like the group. If you are a peer dependent adult, be careful. You will have trouble dealing with questions from those who don't value home education. Can you dare to stand alone on conviction?

*The Big Scare Word— "**Socialization**"*

The educational establishment uses lots of jargon (as any career group tends to do). But sometimes that jargon is deliberately used to intimidate, and nowhere is this more clear than with the word "socialization." If our youngsters aren't with all the other little ones in elementary school (or kindergarten, or playschool, etc.) we're warned that they're missing out on important "socialization" skills.

In Dr. Raymond Moore's booklet, **Research and Common Sense Therapies for Our Homes and Schools,** he mixes expertise with a good dose of common-sense.

> *"Parents and educators usually talk about sociability, but neglect to differentiate the kind of sociability they prefer. The child who feels needed, wanted, and depended on at home, sharing responsibilities and chores, is much more likely to develop a sense of self-worth and a stable value system—which is the basic ingredient for a positive sociability. In contrast is the negative sociability that develops when a child surrenders to his peers.*
>
> *[Others] have found that youngsters at least through the fifth and sixth grades (about ages eleven or twelve) who spend more of their elective time with their peers than with their parents generally became dependent on those peers.. this leads to a pervasive pessimism — about themselves, their future, their parents, and even their peers.*
>
> *Here we hardly have the quality of sociability many parents and educators impute to association with many children. Rather there is a loss of self-direction and self-worth and a dependency that breeds learning failure and delinquency."*

(Another expert, Otto Weininger, points out that children who remain home longer are more likely to demonstrate emotional well-being. They all conclude that peer dependence is the most destructive force in today's schools. And that peer dependence occurs in direct proportion to the number of hours spent with peers and how early that time was spent.)

Dr. Moore concludes that positive socialization occurs when children care for the needs of the elderly or care for the needs of those who are less fortunate than themselves or for the sick.

True positive socialization is passing on our values, standards, and Godly patterns of conduct to the next generation. And we as parents will probably do a much better job with that challenge than the 23 other pre-schoolers in daycare!

The Last Word

All these reasons sound good, but ultimately, who has the last word on your decision? When problems arise mid-school year, remembering academic and social benefits won't carry you through the storm. *The baby is crying, the laundry is piled high, two toddlers are fist fighting, and there's nothing planned for supper. Who said this was a good idea, anyway?* There is only one way to make it through those trials and that is to have developed a conviction that this is, indeed, God's word to your particular family. Did God tell you to homeschool?

Let's close this section with a few scriptures to savor. Let these penetrate into your heart and allow the Holy Spirit to minister to your spirit.

- Proverbs 24:3 ....*Through wisdom a house is built.*

- Proverbs 2:6 ......*For the Lord gives wisdom, out of his mouth come knowledge and understanding.*

- Psalm 119:98 .....*Your commandments make me wiser than my enemies; for Your words are ever before me.*

- Psalm 90:12 ....*So teach us to number our days that we may apply our hearts to wisdom.*

- 2 Peter 1:5 ....*And beside this, giving all diligence, add to your faith virtue, and to virtue knowledge.*

- 2 Timothy 4:3-4 *For the time is coming when people will collect for themselves teachers who will tell them what they are itching to hear; they will turn away from listening to truth and give their attention to legends.*

- Matthew 18:6 ....*But whoso shall offend one of these little ones who believe in me, it were better for him that a mill-stone were hanged around his neck and he were drowned in the depth of the sea.*

- Isaiah 54:13 ....*And all of your children shall be disciples, taught of the Lord and obedient to his will. And great shall be the peace and undisturbed composure of your children.*

Notes:

In this chapter...

- ## Why try?

- ## The nuts and bolts— planning and organizing for success

- ## How to be sure you've covered all the bases.

Rev. 920114

Section One, Chapter Two
Planning for Success

Look carefully at how you walk! Live purposefully, as wise people; making the most of the time, buying up each opportunity, for the days are evil. —Eph. 5:15-16

Thursday morning. 10:30 am.
Spring, 1979.
Turning Point.

I am standing at the kitchen sink. Television is on in the background. A favorite Christian talk show host has just brought up a fascinating subject and I become mesmerized. Beds are unmade. Three-year-old (my oldest) is busy at the kitchen counter with a bowl of cheerios. Dirty breakfast dishes wait on countertop. Telephone rings. *"Gayle,"* my best friend, Lyn, asks, *"have you been watching...just thought you'd want to turn it on."* We talk for 20 minutes. Phone call is finished. I give in and watch the last 30 minutes of the program. Glance at watch. *Yikes! It's almost lunchtime and I'm still in my bathrobe!* The baby's crying to be nursed. Guilt overtakes me and I begin to sob with the baby.

What? Me homeschool? When would I ever do the grocery shopping? I can't even allow a stray visitor to approach my house before midafternoon. How could I be ready to homeschool in the morning? The situation looks hopeless.

Tears flood my cheeks, but I grit my teeth and resolve: *Today I will begin to change.* **Goal:** *to have a home where we can welcome surprise visitors and not be ashamed. To set habit patterns that will allow me to get through the routine housework and give me time for what is really important, like homeschooling.* **I resolve:** *to force myself to develop habits that will keep our home running smoothly,* (Do making the beds and cleaning the bathrooms have to be major events or can they become as habitual and effortless as brushing my teeth?), *to pare my life down to the essentials* (there's too much stuff to take care of around here), *so I can spend more time on people than things.*

The pain of being disorganized had become more than I could take. I was not born organized (certainly) but I was born with a desire to become organized. Were there really enough minutes in the day or did God make a mistake when he created 24 hour days?

After that kitchen counter experience, in my time with the Lord, I came to three major conclusions over a period of a few weeks.

First, our family needed a focus. What was the one big calling or purpose God had for us? Homeschoolers believe that we are called to operate as a unit, not several fragmented parts going in many directions at once.

I know a local family that everyone calls creative. If you want some fun ideas for ministry or a party, go to them. Their ideas are usually affordable, too. The Coopers here in town are known as merciful. They are always remembering the sick or elderly with a helping hand. (They also have adopted three older children.) Then there are the Copes — they're known as hospitable. Always a hot pot of coffee and some fresh pastry ready for you in their home. Better not want to leave early when you visit them, either. People are important to them. What did God want the world to say about the Grahams? Surely, God had a special word for our family description, too. And He has one for you!

The second conclusion was that I needed to view myself as an executive home manager who answers to the Chief Executive Officer and not as a slave (a servant, yes, but not a slave.) What does an executive manager do? She directs, plans, and coordinates those who are in her charge. (Sometimes she has to tell the CEO where *he* has to be, too.) A manager trains and motivates those under her, too. A manager teaches others to serve by her example. She doesn't just tell, she shows. She doesn't just expect, she inspects. She must be the hardest worker on the team, but she's also constantly encouraging others to do their jobs well.

An executive home manager reports to her boss, the Chief Executive Officer, the father. (Single Moms report directly to the Heavenly Father.) My children needed to see that I answered to a higher authority who was overseeing this whole operation. He wasn't going to decide what we ate for breakfast or when it was time for new tennis shoes, and he probably wasn't going to be flashing many vocabulary cards to the children, but he was going to oversee the enterprise.

The third thing I learned (and these became convictions) was that it was time to ruthlessly weed distractors. There are two main categories of distractors— *material* distractors and *time* distractors.

Rev. 9201

Material distractors

Material distractors require energy to maintain. Clutter zaps our mental energy. One whole kitchen cabinet in my kitchen was devoted to plastic storage containers, most of them rarely used. Ziplock bags would take less storage space and could be reused repeatedly. Round containers were discarded for square and rectangular ones, which take up less space. The fancy juicer I rarely used was given to a friend who needed to drink carrot juice for her allergies. The list could go on. Suffice it to say, I found two large plastic trashbags full of stuff I really didn't need in the kitchen.

It didn't stop there. Not only did gadgets in the kitchen have to go, but clothing had to be sorted, discarded, and given away. I wanted half empty drawers and closets for all of us. Anything not used in the last calendar year was given away even if I still liked it! That meant fewer choices for me to make in the morning and I was happy about it. My husband sometimes misses the good sweaters of his I gave away, but I comfort myself by knowing that someone who was cold needed those sweaters more than we did. By the way, I also got rid of the extra work shoe my husband was saving. That's right, we both laugh about the 'one *pair* plus one *spare*' loafer he was saving "just in case". (He sheepishly tells me he ruined the match to the spare by spilling gasoline on it but saved the extra shoe "just in case".)

We hit the utility storage area, too. For example, old paint cans were discarded and numbers of the paint colors were written in my home management notebook for reference. Children's toys were given away or sent to the attic for periodic retrieval and exchange. Less is best for them, too. How can the typical American child keep up with all his stuff?

(I'm convinced that material distraction is one of the main reasons we Christians don't always have a Sabbath. We are so mentally confused by clutter and busy on the weekends maintaining what we have that we can't see our way clear to plan for a Sabbath. I am saying this from unfortunate personal experience.)

Time distractors

I was playing tennis 3 days per week for exercise. I found I could walk 3 miles each day and get more exercise in one half the time. I made the trade. Meal preparation could be a real time-robber. I researched how to cook nutritious meals in the crockpot and how to double and freeze recipes. Now on Sunday nights, I jump start all of the week's food preparation. Soups are started, vegetables sliced and stored, muffins cooked. The kitchen has one major cleanup and much smaller cleanups during the week that way. Dinner preparation is a snap on the days I have the least energy.

WHAT'S YOUR JOB DESCRIPTION?

What's your job description?
Wife? Mother? Teacher? *All of the above? Don't lose sight of it, whatever it is.*

One February morning I listened to the weather forecast. For three days we were expected to have sunny skies and temperatures in the 80's. Hot dog! Time to get outside and paint those windows! Money was short and the windows were really bugging me. In three days I could probably paint all the mullions across the front of the house. I planned unsupervised schoolwork for the children and was on my way!

Painting takes longer than I thought. Going around all those little panes is not as easy as it looks. After six hours on one window I realized I would have to hurry before the rains arrived in three days.

There I was, hanging out of the second story window, painting away. Children needed spelling words called. Not to worry — I called them from the windowsill. The phone rang. Homeschool mother in trouble. Needed a few encouraging words.

Back to the painting. Oops! My two-year-old had tried to paint a window while I was gone. Better grab some paint remover fast! Telephone rang again.

This went on for two days. Time grew short and rain was in the forecast. Suddenly something occurred to me while hanging from the porch roof(easy access to bedroom windows). My husband was downtown in his office working. He was not supervising toddlers while he worked. He wasn't answering the telephone except as it pertained to his job.
*What was **my** job description?*

I jumped from the roof into the open window and raced to the telephone to call a professional painter. "Please come now. This is an emergency! One half of our windows are white and the other half blue. How fast can you paint?"

To make a long story short, the painter was booked for six weeks but he finally came and finished the job. Meanwhile, my neighbors suffered while they looked at our blue and white windows. One commented that all I needed was an American flag and I would be ready for President's Day. Quite a patriotic sight!

*But I learned a lesson I will never forget. My job description is **wife / mother / teacher.** There are some things I just don't do because I am homeschooling.*

And that's okay.

Rev. 9201

Housework was definitely taking too much time. How could I build relationships with my children if I was cleaning all day? I decided to spend only one hour per day on routine house cleaning in the morning. Not more. (Removing and putting away clutter is not house cleaning. I also set a goal of not going to bed at night with a cluttered home.)

I divided the chores that needed to be done throughout the week into five days, keeping in mind that the time I had to spend on this was only one hour. We established a comfort level and now try to maintain that daily. Major cleaning projects (like window washing) have to be a family affair on Saturdays or be done on teacher inservice days. (By the way, the dust doesn't bother us nearly as much as the clutter used to.) As the children have grown older, they have taken over the maintenance chores, freeing me up to train younger children and oversee (inspect) the whole operation.

Juggling it all takes a toll in both time and mental energy. Being a Mom — especially a homeschool Mom — requires we master demands on our time. We must see the big picture before trying to fill in details. Too often, we tend to start with details (like which math workbook to purchase) before looking at the big picture (I will teach math over the course of years!)

Looking at a weekly schedule sheet (**Mom's Week at a Glance**, pgs. 30-32) with the days of the week across the top and times of the day along the side helps me see how I'm doing in balancing priorities. *Are we sticking with what is important?* I fill in the must-do's first, then highlight where I'll be at any given time and write in generally what each child is doing (*'seatwork'*, not *'reading, p.33'*.) Seeing this on paper shows me I cannot be in two places at once and that I don't have time for every workbook every single day.

I have about 8 years to teach my children before they reach high school. I do not need to model my homeschool after a public school which isolates and teaches every subject every day. Pray to see priorities. My personal motto: **Do what I can with the time that I have!**

What was I really after? I desired so much to have a home where anyone could drop in unexpectedly, where we would be able to welcome that person into our home and not be ashamed. (I said that once, didn't I?) If I could get the broad picture first: family focus, viewing my role as an executive home manager, and weeding distractors, I would be on my way to filling in the details of being a homeschool Mom.

HOUSEHOLD CHORES — WEEK AT A GLANCE

Routines reduce stress.
"What do I need to do each day in order to maintain my acceptable standard of cleanliness?"
Break larger chores into smaller chunks (ex. instead of 'dusting entire house', dust 2 rooms per day.
Or instead of having one child do the bathroom, have one do the toilet and floor,
another the shower, and another the sink and mirror.)

Chores:

Monday:
Change linens.
Clean refrigerator.

Tuesday:
Iron.
Dust downstairs.
Clean schoolroom.

Wednesday:
Clean mirrors.
Wipe woodwork, cabinets

Thursday:
Kitchen & utility floors
Shake rugs.

Friday:
Sweep porches & stairs.
Clean desk tops.
Dust upstairs.

Saturday:
Yardwork.
Car.
Vacuum. (DAD♡)

Daily:

Laundry.
Wipe down bathrooms.
Kitchen: floor - Heather
counters - Ashley
sink, pans - Amy

Remove junk/trash from
bedroom each day -- ALL!

**Material Distractors
to eliminate**
GOAL: De-clutter each night!
Dejunk weekly - one room!

**Time Distractors
to eliminate**

Remember to put on the
answering machine!

**Monitor the use of your time...
Are you spending it as you desire?**
Spend time w/ Lee!

Organization and Goals

Prayer plus planning equals progress. Most of us avoid planning. We're understandably anxious to dig into those teacher's manuals, buy that curriculum, order those books and start teaching. But before we start to build a homeschool, it is vital that we lay a solid foundation.

Knowing why you're homeschooling is a starting point, like an artist's rendering of the new building you want to begin. Planning gives you the blueprints. Do we ever have to change our plans? Of course. Blueprints are always being revised. But I wouldn't want to build (or live in) a house without one!

Organization

Getting organized is a homeschool prerequisite. As a homeschool Mom, you'll be overseeing several operations at once — *mothering, teaching, homemaking* — so you'll need to be organized in order to think clearly. And your children will need to learn organizational skills from you. What I'd like to do is help you get organized to have a smoothly run homeschool.

Reasons to be organized

It is useless to set goals that cannot be met. It will be very difficult to meet educational goals if your home is not organized, your materials are not organized, and your thoughts are not organized.

Organized households provide time for that which is important. If our households are organized, we will have many, many more hours of time for more important things like homeschooling.

Disorganization spells discomfort. Have you ever gone to the front door to meet an unannounced visitor and felt like you couldn't let them inside? That isn't how we want our children to feel when they're home with us for school. We want to enjoy visitors, to be able to allow people into our homes without embarrassment.

Organization is a catalyst for peace, order, and tranquility in our homes. I remember a babysitter I once had for my young children. This babysitter was my children's favorite because she was so much fun. But when I'd come home, every game, every toy, every art supply would be out and nothing put away after being used.

One day I came home to a totalled house — a wreck. I felt peace leave as I walked into the room (my children were a little on the hyper side, too.) Well, we have a saying in our house that there is a home for every object and sometimes we have to help things find their homes— so we did! Once that was done, peace returned. There was tranquility again. We could enjoy life together.

Look carefully at how you walk! Live purposefully, as wise people; making the most of the time, buying up each opportunity, for the days are evil. — Eph. 5:15-16

A disorganized woman has a low self-esteem.. She can't be the person God has called her to be, because she is so burdened.

Academic benefits. An organized student has organized thinking and this pays off in all subject areas. Whether in math, reading comprehension, report writing or study skills, an organized student will have organized thinking. If your child can organize his closet, he can organize a paper. Next time your mother-in-law calls on a school day and you and the children are having a "tidy attack" organizing closets and she asks what you're doing— just tell her *"I'm teaching writing skills."*

Taking control of household chores

What are some ways we can minimize the time needed for basics such as housework so we'll have more time for the important things in life? Let's take another look at how to tackle those two villains that complicate our lives — *material distractors* and *time distractors.*

Eliminating Material Distractors
We need to take at least two weeks prior to the beginning of our school for de-cluttering.

Think: Fewer is best. Sort your children's clothing drawers. A child does not need to have 10 pairs of socks and 15 pairs of under-wear, or 8 pairs of jeans and 10 shirts. Select a few of the best for your needs. Give the others away to someone who has a need. Five outfits is enough. Half-empty drawers stay more orderly. Young children can organize clothing if it is kept in small plastic baskets, one for each category. For example, all socks go into one basket, underwear in another, etc. Clean closets should be a pre-requisite for starting homeschooling.

Clean and sort. Eliminate the extras. My first step in repentance after that kitchen counter experience was to thoroughly go through each area of the house. I had garbage bags filled with junk I didn't really need. When you do this, be ruthless!

Hint: Would you like more money for homeschool materials? Gather all the things you haven't used in the last year. All the maternity clothes from years past. All the things that you will never use or *that someone else could use if it weren't hidden in your closet.* Then have a yard sale! (When I gathered together my junk, I had everything from ancient waffle irons to 6" ties from my husband's college days.)

No matter how much (or how little) money you make, you'll be glad you de-junked. Your time is valuable. The more you get rid of, the less time you have to spend maintaining what you do have.

Rev. 920114

While you're at it, make the children's rooms work for them. For example, use low shelves and bars for hanging clothes that they can reach. Sort young children's folded clothing into baskets on a low shelf in a closet rather than in cumbersome drawers. Think about how your children can be responsible for everything that is theirs. (Part of homeschooling is teaching responsiblity, *right*?)

Eliminating Time Distractors
Housework can be a great time distractor. While it is not a priority to be a fanatic about housekeeping, your home can be well maintained within reasonable time-constraints.

(If anything, your home will begin to look better when you start homeschooling. You will be forced to be more organized. You will be forced to start using your children's help with the house. And you will want to finish your housework early in the morning to be ready for homeschool.)

What are some specific things we can do to minimize time needed for housework?

At the beginning of the day, take time to care for yourself. Be sure your children know that once they wake up, they, too, should care for their personal needs. The children dress, their rooms are straight, their hair is brushed, their beds are made — all of this before they ever come to the kitchen for breakfast. If all your children are under five, this will take some time because they are still in training. If you have lots of children of mixed ages, pair an older child with a younger one for the morning routine. Young or untrained children will spend a good part of your first homeschool year assimilating these morning habits. Work on them and allow yourself the time in the morning to train your children. Training is a valid part of your homeschool day and will reap you hours later on.

For the home, plan and establish a daily routine of cleanliness. (Work this out, in pencil of course, on a copy of the **Housekeeping Worksheet** from Appendix C.) For example, each morning have a general pick-up time and eliminate all the excess baggage. Have daily, not just weekly, cleaning times.

If you clean daily, you will actually save time in the long run. So, decide how you want your house to look, how clean you want it to be and plan to maintain it daily. Daily chores might include sweeping, cleaning the bathroom, doing laundry, wiping counter-tops, preliminary dinner preparation. Think of maintenance cleaning as a daily routine rather than waiting for major massive cleaning days.

GETTING IT ALL DONE

Yearly (Before school starts):
1. List all breakfasts, dinners on master list for quick future reference when planning menus and grocery shopping lists.

2. Do a major clean-up of house.

3. Take a family clothing inventory.
   Needs will surface. (ex.: no blouse for this skirt.) Discard extras. List absolute needs in your home management notebook.
   (ex.: Meg does not have a winter coat.)

Monthly:
Make one major trip to grocery store.
Stock up on staples, canned goods, non-perishables.

When to grocery shop:
1. Very early before starting school.

2. During dinner hour while husband feeds children.

3. Whenever you can get a babysitter.

When not to grocery shop:
1. Thursday or Friday night.

2. Saturday

3. When you have more than one child with you.

De-junk one day per month, at least. Be ruthless. Give away. Throw away. Sell.

Weekly:
Sunday - Worship and rest.
   Enjoy your family and the freedom to do whatever restores you.

Sunday night - Look over schedule for the week.
Be sure to communicate scheduling, commitments for the week with husband.
Start meal preparation (ex.-Slice and store carrot sticks for lunches.
Prepare soups or casseroles ahead. Cook and freeze breakfast pancakes.)

Monday - Tuesday - Wednesday - Thursday - Friday—
Do daily maintenance cleaning for one hour in morning.
Be sure to go to bed with a straight house.

Friday— Do lesson planning in the afternoon for the next week.

Saturday—Major household projects day.
   Shopping (not grocery)

Saturday at sundown—Prepare yourself and family for church. Begin your Sabbath.

Rev. 9201

Use your children to help with this! With your children's help, you can take one hour per day to maintain your home. Organize your children's chores. They will do your housework if you break it down into small chunks they can handle. In our house, the seven-year-old cleans the toilet each day (among other things). Her older sister cleans the bathroom floor and the next older cleans the bathroom sink and counter each day. *Voila!* A clean bathroom each day.

For those of you whose oldest is under seven, you need help. Help from your husband or a neighbor's teenage daughter or other source. Children under seven are in training and not the assets they will one day be to your home routine.

To help your children get used to this sort of routine include their chores on their assignment sheets (which I will explain later.) At first, plan your child's day minute by minute until the routine that you expect is established. If you do this, everything will eventually run smoothly.

For children who are not accustomed to this sort of lifestyle, you are actually going to have to plan step by step and minute by minute how their mornings will be spent. Train your children, working with them through daily chores repeatedly before launching them on their own. Inspect often!

From time to time, you might enjoy reading some of the many good motivational books available on organization and goals. At the end of this chapter, I've listed a few of the books that have encouraged me over the years.

HOME MANAGEMENT NOTEBOOK

Daytimer / dayplanner that you can make all your own...

1. **Appointment calendar**

2. **Telephone and address directory**

3. **"To-do" pages**

4. **Customizable for personalized sections**
   (menu plans, clothes, gift plans, Sunday School notes, etc.)

SCHOOL MANAGEMENT NOTEBOOK

Keep the following in a loose-leaf notebook:

1. **Program of Study for each child, as well as Curriculum Scope pages to record basic subjects and unit topics the child has covered in each grade.**

2. **Mom's Week at a Glance scheduling page.**

3. **Coordinating a number of children page (for large families.)**

4. **Yearly Goal Sheet (see Appendix C)**

5. **Monthly Goal Sheet (see Appendix C)**

6. **Week at a Glance Assignment sheets for each child. (Copy about 36 per child.)**

7. **Weekly unit study planning sheets. (one per week for Mom's unit lesson plans)**

8. **Records of annual achievement testing. (You may prefer to keep these in a separate file.)**

Rev. 92011

Management Tools for Home and School

Homeschool recordkeeping need not be complex. If we save our energy on recordkeeping, we'll have more time for our real job — teaching our children! I'm suggesting a streamlined recordkeeping system with just three basic components: a *home* management notebook, *school* management notebook, and *child's* notebook.

Home Management Notebook

As an effective home manager, you'll need a portable daytimer/dayplanner to keep up with your logistics (as well as everyone else's, *right*?) Look for one with an appointment calendar, daily or weekly to-do pages, an address and telephone number directory, and space to add your own personalized sections (Bible study, Christmas section, birthdays, personal yellow pages for frequently called businesses, Sunday school notes, etc.)

You might include a gift buying section where you list presents as they are bought ahead. Keep a list of family clothing needs and sizes so that when you buy, it will not be an impulse purchase. Also helpful is a menu planning section with space for a grocery list, so that as you plan your week's or month's menus, you can simultaneously make a grocery list. Make this home management notebook suit *your* style.

This is your *home* management tool. Don't try to use this to keep up with school management too, or you'll just overload it. (This is *not* where you'll plan your school day — we'll come to that notebook next.)

Choose a format small enough to carry with you wherever you go. Next time you're out for a dental appointment and make a new appointment in six months, you can write it directly into your calendar and *not have to fool around with that little card that will surely get lost*. Or when you see a friend in the grocery store who asks you about switching a meeting time you can jot it down (or resolve the conflict with another appointment) right on the spot. *Less stress!*

Information written down is information you can put out of your mind until needed. This automatically reduces the stress associated with a busy life.

School Management Notebook

The school management notebook is a looseleaf binder which includes all the various details, plans and schedules that Mom needs as teacher/administrator. (See summary on opposite page.) Perhaps the best starting point is each child's **Program of Study** (forms in Appendix C). When planning a program of study for your child for the coming school year, look first at your goals in

- Sample -

Curriculum Scope (K-8) for: *Heather Graham*				
Year	Reading	Written Language	Math	Units
1989-1990	phonic readers phonic manual Library	phonic dictation language exp. Letter cubes	CCP Text B Pre Math It Kit	Human Body Children of the World States, Regions Continents, Geography
1990-1991	phonic readers AlphaPhonics EASY READERS Library	Explode the Code phonic spelling italic writing dictation	MTP-mwm B Math It Kit	Explorers -Colonists Indians -frontier life Impressionists Artists Electricity - Magnetism
1991-1992	fluent readers library reading for unit	Lang. Exp. LLATL-Yellow italic -C indv. Spelling	MTP-mwm B Math It Kit	Plants Animals Military / Flight + Floating Australia Honor- God + Man

reading, written language, math, and unit studies. Then select appropriate materials to use in those four major areas, balancing your choices. (We'll be talking about just how to do that throughout much of the remainder of this book.)

Next comes your set of curriculum scope pages to record the subjects covered in each school year for a particular child. (I've included a sample here, with blank forms in Appendix C). On this sheet, you list year by year any textbooks used, and the subjects or unit topics covered in a particular grade.

This will give you a continuum. You can look at the past to see where you have been. You can look at the future to see where you are going. It also helps you when you have younger children coming behind the older ones. You can look back and see, "*Now what did I cover with my oldest child when he was in the sixth grade? What materials did I use for beginning reading instruction? Have I done a constellation unit? How old was my third child when we did that? Is it time to go back and do it again?*" This will give a long-range scope of where you have been and where you are going — the yearly big picture for school.

In your loose-leaf school notebook, you should also have a weekly overview page (I call mine ***Mom's Week at a Glance***) with the days of the week across the top of a page and the hours of the day down the side. Fill in unchangeables like tutoring sessions, music lessons, co-op days first.

At major planning times (beginning of school year, etc.) use this sheet as a place to work out your own master schedule. *When will you plan to tutor that beginning reader? When will you spend time with the toddlers and what will the older children be doing at that time? How will it all fit?*

Use pencil— you'll want to revise your plan along the way. It's very likely that your schedule will need occasional revision as your family changes and grows. (*If you're like me at all, your schedule will change several times in September!*)

While as a Mom you can't set your plans in concrete, filling out a sheet like this allows you to see the weekly big picture on one page. Create your own, suitable schedule. Relieve stress by setting routines that make sense for your family. Try to balance your choices for the week. You'll automatically see that you cannot be in two places at once. Hold yourself accountable for the hours in the week and nothing more.

Your schedule will be unique. There are as many different schedules as there are homeschools. I've included some examples over the next few pages, but these are only samples.

MOM'S WEEK AT A GLANCE

	Monday	Tuesday	Wednesday	Thursday	Friday
6:00					
6:30	⟵——— Wake up		Wake up ———⟶		
7:00	⟵——— FAMILY EATS BREAKFAST ———⟶				
7:30	⟵— Older Children leave for School —⟶				
8:00					
8:30	} Housework, Phone Calls, etc. {				
9:00					
9:30					
10:00					
10:30	Mom teach basics:				
11:00	READING, WRITTEN LANGUAGE,				
11:30	MATH				
NOON	⟵— Lunch		Lunch —⟶		
12:30					
1:00	Work	ERRANDS	Work	ART CLASS	Visit library
1:30	on	&	on		
2:00	Unit theme	SHOPPING	unit theme		
2:30	together.		together.		
3:00					
Late Aft.					
Dinner					
After Dinner					

Sample Schedule A — *This mother is teaching her 8 year-old at home.*
There are teenagers in the family attending school outside the home.

© Gayle Graham (from the "How to Home School" Manual)

MOM'S WEEK AT A GLANCE

	Monday	Tuesday	Wednesday	Thursday	Friday
6:00					
6:30					
7:00	←Wake up, Dress, Walk carefully				
7:30	through morning routine together →				
8:00	←Breakfast and Bible reading.→				
8:30					
9:00	←"Chores," especially orderliness→				
9:30	Mom start dinner. Children listen to tapes, play.				
10:00	Mom teach 6 yr. old. Toddler in room for				
10:30	1 hr. playtime. Infant naps.				
11:00	All walk, play outside.				
11:30					
NOON	←—Lunch - Lunch - Lunch→				
12:30					
1:00					
1:30	Read aloud to toddler.				
2:00	Teach 6yr. old while baby and toddler				
2:30	nap.				
3:00					
Late Aft.					
Dinner					
After Dinner					

Sample Schedule B — *This mother has one 6 year-old, one toddler, & one baby. She needs husband or helper for heavy housework.*

MOM'S WEEK AT A GLANCE

	Monday	Tuesday	Wednesday	Thursday	Friday
6:00	← Mom and Dad waken. Quiet Time. Exercise →				
6:30					
7:00	← Children awake. Dress. Rooms straightened. →				
7:30	← Breakfast and Bible. →				
8:00	Chores	Chores	Chores	Chores	Chores
8:30	← Older Children Quiet Time. (Mom with toddlers.) →				
9:00	← Older children French, Latin. →			ALL HANDS-ON LEARNING DAY! NO BOOKS!	↑ French tutor here! ↓
9:30					
10:00	Mom teaches Ashley in Library.	Group Time: Unit Reading			Group Time. Follow up for week!
10:30					
11:00					
11:30					
NOON	Lunch	Lunch	Lunch		Lunch
12:30	← Mom read to toddlers... →				...
1:00	Mom teach basics to Amy, Heather while toddlers nap. Seatwork follow-up.				Mom teach Writing Club.
1:30					
2:00					
2:30					Algebra tutor ↑↓
3:00					
Late Aft.	Swim team	Swim team			swim team
Dinner			CHURCH		
After Dinner	← Dad reads aloud! →		CHURCH	Same →	Family Night!

Busy Mom Schedule! *As your family grows, scheduling will become more complex—older children have special classes, tutors, sports, etc. How will you juggle it all? Use pencil!*

© Gayle Graham (from the "How to Home School" Manual)

LARGE FAMILY SUGGESTIONS

1. Some large families start their school day at staggered times.

2. Conquer a unit in the summer. ex.: "Summer of Science"— all hands-on!

3. Individualize only math and language arts. Teach all ages the same units in science or history, and vary assignments.

4. Accomplish 5 days of academics in four days, taking one day off for field trips, crafts, experiments, etc.

5. Let older children spend one hour each morning "teaching" toddlers while you teach younger beginning readers. If the older child prepares lessons for the toddler related to the unit of study he'll learn even more or...

6. In the morning, let the oldest child teach the other older children a subject he is slightly ahead in but could use repetition on (such as a foreign language, grammar, or spelling), while you spend the first part of the day with the baby or toddler.

7. Work like Trojans for six weeks, taking the seventh for family activities. Set goals ahead and be specific!

8. Plan daily how you will divide the time you have among your children. Have a specific idea of when you will be with each child and for how long. Remember, you are only one person, a human being. God will stretch your time and make the minutes count! (See "Coordinating a Number of Children" and weekly planning pages.)

Sanity Breaks

Feeling frustrated with your schedule? You probably just need a teacher in-service day. When the walls start caving in and you feel like you're going to collapse, you probably just need to regroup. Take a cleaning and sorting day. Have a tidy attack. Once the house is back in order, you'll feel renewed. All teachers have in-service days. Plan to give yourself six or eight each schoolyear.

When planning your weekly and daily schedules, consider: Are you allowing yourself the luxury of a daily quiet time? I'm told that John Wesley's mother got her quiet time by placing an apron over her head. The children knew not to interrupt her private time when that apron was over her head!

Maybe you'd prefer a daily prayer walk outside. Alone. Or, perhaps a warm nightly bath is more your style. We all need a release. Plan for it!

By the way...

What's your alternate schedule?

When your family has been up late the night before attending that special church event, it might not be realistic to expect everyone to get up early. Plan for those days with an alternate schedule:

ALTERNATE SCHEDULE:

8:30 Wake up

9:00 Breakfast, Chores

10:00 French study together

11:00 Unit Time with family

12:30 Lunch

1:00 - 4:00 Finish assignments.

Rev. 92011

Every family is growing. Your schedule will be different from every homeschooling family you know. Just decide your routines and set down your schedule in writing so you can focus your mental energy on more important things.

Coordinating a Number of Children
If you have a large family, the third thing you will need in your school management notebook is a master plan of how you will coordinate your children. Some families tell me they start their school day at staggered times. This makes for a longer day for the Mom, but it might work for you. Other families might start their school year at staggered times. For example, the year I was having another baby, I started my kindergartener early in August anticipating that she would have time off when the baby arrived in January.

(By the way, you might want to conquer a unit during summer. Summer is a great time to study outdoors. You could do insects, pond life, butterflies. The list is endless. Have a summer of science, say a summer of life science, and conquer a unit ahead of time.)

Large families generally individualize only in language arts and math, teaching all the other ages the same units in science, history, etc. Many also plan to accomplish five days of academics in four days, taking the middle day (Wednesday) off for field trips, crafts, experiments etc. (*Quite a motivator!*)

Large families also find it helpful at times to use the older ones to teach the younger ones. This is especially good if the skill is one that the older one has just learned and needs reinforcing. This helps the older child as well as the younger one.

Sometimes large families will work especially hard for six weeks doing seven weeks worth of assignments and taking the seventh week for just family activities.

To use creative approaches like these, you need to set specific goals ahead of time and be thoughtful as you plan. For example, it is helpful to teach science one semester and history another semester rather than doing the two subjects at the same time. That makes less planning for you and less confusion for your child.

Plan daily how you will divide your day between the children, having a specific idea of when you will be with each child and for how long. Expect changes in this ideal plan and do the best you can with the time you have.

COORDINATING A NUMBER OF CHILDREN — MASTER PLAN AT-A-GLANCE

Name:	Ashley (13)	Amy (10)	Heather (6)	Meg (infant)
8:30	Quiet Time	Quiet Time	Quiet Time	Mom with Meg
9:00	Latin ↓	Composition ↓	Mom teach phonics and math.	Am nap ↓
9:30				
10:00	Algebra ↓	Mom teach Spelling grammar vocabulary math or dictation	seatwork	Play in room w/ gate
10:30			play with Meg ↓	
11:00	Mom teach: composition, literature	Seatwork ↓		
11:30	prepare lunch		free time	Mom walks with Meg.
12:00	Lunch	Lunch	Lunch	Lunch
12:30	Writing, literature			
1:00	Reading related to units.	Assigned reading.	Assigned reading.	Mom read to Meg.
2:00	typing			Nap
After Dinner	Swim team practice	swim team practice	Dad read aloud.	Play with Dad.

Note: This is a rotating daily schedule for large families. Use four days per week only.
One day can be hands-on, project day!

As you can see, if you have a large family, you will need a written master schedule of how you will coordinate your children on a *daily* basis (kept in your handy School Management Notebook, of course.) *Include all of your children, even the baby and the toddler on this schedule.* (See "**Coordinating a Number of Children**" sample on the next page. Blank forms are included in Appendix C. *If you're a Mom who finds this sheet helpful, I probably don't need to remind you to use pencil.*)

Highlight when you will spend time with each child. For example, with my children, I plan to rotate, starting each day with the youngest child. Give the younger ones lots of attention (until they are ready to leave you.) Older childen can be doing chores or starting on the schoolday with something they can handle without you.

Our day begins with the oldest child teaching French and vocabulary to the next two in line while I focus on the two-year-old and four-year-old. Usually the younger ones get tired of me after about 45 minutes and are ready to play alone for awhile. Later, a mid-morning snack and outdoor playtime help the younger ones last until lunchtime.

The infant also has a playpen period. As I finish with one child, I move on to the next and I try to spend a designated time with her. In between, I know what the other children will be working on and I have an idea of whether it will be something that they need pre-teaching in or something they can handle alone. *Schedule concentrated teaching times (ex. teaching a six-year-old to read) while the baby and toddler nap.*

My hope is to have a few individual minutes of instruction each day with each child.

Did you notice the words "TRY" and "HOPE"? That is exactly what a written schedule is supposed to help me do. If you think for one minute that I am humanly able to stick religiously to my plan for the day, you are wrong. But the Holy Spirit is my children's real teacher and I am His servant. I am only required to do what I can with the time and faculties He has given me, nothing more. Remember the Motto? **DO WHAT YOU CAN WITH THE TIME THAT YOU HAVE!**

The fourth thing you will want for your school management notebook is *a record of weekly individual assignments for each reading child.* (There are **Assignment Week at a Glance** sheets in Appendix C which you may copy for your child's use. These sheets are best for children eight and up who are fluent readers. You might use 32, 36, maybe even 40 sheets for each of your children

ASSIGNMENTS — WEEK AT A GLANCE

Name Amy   **Week of** _____

Subject	Monday	Tuesday	Wednesday	Thursday	Friday
Group Time 8:20-9:00	Mom reads	aloud to all. →→→		Mom reads	aloud to all. ←→
Quiet Time 9:00-9:15	Romans 12:4-8	I Cor. 12:12-26	↑ Projects and Hands-on Learning Day! ↓	Eph. 4:1-6	You choose!
Writing 9:15-10:00	Copy ₮ p.73 Literature	Write about the meaning of cooperation.		Revise Tuesday's Writing.	You decide! Write 30 min.
Time with Mom 10:00-10:45	Mom dictate above. Discuss similes. Math.	Discuss paragraph. Teach math.		Math Spelling Drills.	Math Teach counting change-
Vocab. & Spelling 10:45-11:15	1. cooperation 2. cells 3. microscope 4. organ	1. nucleus 2. cytoplasm 3. organism 4.		Practice test.	Test
Math 11:15-12:00	p.72- all Do "Math It."	p.77 omit 2, 5		p.100-all Practice time, money.	p.269- all p.65- 1-30.
Assigned Reading 1:00	Choose a book from the basket to read.	Same		Label butterflies.	Same
Mom's Notes:	☺ "Remember! Listen to Amy read.			Art lesson: 1:30-2:30	

© Gayle Graham (from the "How to Home School" Manual)

depending on the number of school weeks you plan). On this sheet, record daily assignments for the week. Most Moms like to do this on the weekend prior to the week beginning.

As you gain experience you will be able to plan several weeks at once. It helps me to plan one month of these at a sitting. Then I can see if there is a balance of choices over a period of time. Use pencil, though; you'll be making adjustments. Your child uses this as a checklist.

There are some real benefits for your child in giving him his assignments a week at a glance. They can see from this sheet exactly what to expect for a whole week. If they're motivated, they can try to finish a little bit early by doubling up on assignments when they have extra time. At the end of the week, you collect these sheets and store them in your home school management notebook as a record of the work that they have accomplished. As you can see, this eliminates the need for a teacher's plan book.

Children too young for a weekly assignment sheet do well to have a section for each day of the week in their own 3-ring binder, where you can hole-punch and store each day's papers for the coming week. (More on the child's notebook later.) Get this notebook ready for the week on your planning day.

Unit Plans

You also want a record of the plans for the unit studies that you will be doing corporately with your children. (We'll look at unit studies in detail in Section 3 *"Exploring and Learning Together."* This includes all of the rest after teaching individualized reading, written language, and math lessons to the child.) It's a great idea to teach your children as a group in the same subject area and vary assignments according to the ages and abilities of the children.

For example, if you are studying the explorers, why not study them with all of your children of different ages? What you will do is keep a record of the plans you have made for corporate studies with the children. Usually one page is sufficient for your records for one week. You will record the projects, the experiments you plan to do with your children, the books you will read aloud, and field trips you will take.

Most of the project work you choose to do can be done on the non-academic day. As I mentioned before, many families who choose this unit study approach do academic work three or four days per week, and hands-on discovery/experimental learning one or two days a week. You'll need to decide how much time in academics vs. projects suits your family's needs. You'll also record on that

UNIT PLANS — WEEK AT A GLANCE

Unit Topic: _Human Body - Muscles_   Week # _4_

Reading, Simple Activity

Day 1
  p. 76 - Konos pre-test
  <u>Skin</u> & <u>Bones</u> - Ch. 7

Day 2
  Same - Ch. 7
Ashley draw and teach
major muscles & bones
they cover.

Day 3
<u>Blood</u> & <u>Guts</u> - p. 31

Day 4
Joe's Body - foot/hand
Look at slides of blood
cells. Do bones dittoes.

Hands-on Day!

1. Draw faces with a
variety of expressions.
(muscles)

2. p. 30-32 - Do checked
items in Konos.

3. p. 29- Dissect chicken
   leg (See Blood & Guts
                    p. 46)

4. p. 29 Make a model
      of a muscle.

5. Make and play
a matching game of
muscles and bones.

Trips?

Visit a seesaw.
        (p. 30 - Konos)

Supply List

for Wednesday:
  3 cardboard rolls
  3 rubber bands
  paper clips
  2 long balloons
  chicken legs (not cut)

Comments

* Chicken leg dissection
was a real hit. At the
end, girls played classical
music and watched
the legs "dance"
          Yuk!

Sit down and do a whole unit of these at one time. (Use pencil.)
On four days, plan to read and do simple activities. Save one day for experiments, projects, etc.

sheet lists of materials to gather and books you hope to find in the library. So, you can see that this sheet is your personalized planning sheet for the unit of the week.

Many families are now joining together in the summer to prepare topics to be studied during the school year. Moms plan and co-op their projects, giving them more free time and a chance to really plan a dynamite unit for the group when it's their turn.

One final note, you will want to keep records of annual achievement testing either in this notebook or perhaps in your important papers file.

Child's Notebook
The last component in our management system is the Child's Notebook. Using a 3-ring binder with notebook dividers, keep one section for each unit as it is studied, plus a section for math, spelling, foreign language, or other specifics you are studying. Sample papers are kept in each section. (De-clutter weekly.)

For example, say you are doing a unit on the human body. You might investigate a cow's kidney, write a report about Robert Hook (who discovered cells), draw a diagram of the eye, or take a snapshot while on a field trip to the local hospital lab. Include all of that in the section of your notebook entitled Human Body. Perhaps your child writes an imaginary story about a voyage through the circulatory system or reads a biography of Louis Pasteur. Include these also in the Human Body unit section.

Other things you might want to include in your child's notebook include a copy of the goals set for the school year, a cumulative list of great books as they are read (see **Great Books Registry** form in Appendix C), a writing checklist of skills to remember when proofing papers, or a daily and weekly schedule sheet. The point is to keep it simple and make it his personal record.

What about projects too large for the binder? Photograph them and then donate them to charity in the wee hours of the night.

No more clutter! No more loose, flying papers! Your children will have less busy work as homeschoolers and the papers and records they keep will be more meaningful. *Paper production does not equal good schooling*!

Whew! How much time does all this planning take? It takes approximately one and one-half hours per week of planning time alone to coordinate your school and home management notebooks, and to fill in the children's assignment sheets. (Double this time the first month you try it.) In time, you'll find planning becomes a routine, taking only a few minutes a day.

Think of planning time as an investment. The time you spend planning will be more than repaid to you in accomplishment during your school week. I recommend that first-year homeschool Moms spend half a day per week outside of the home for reflection and planning. This can be spent in the library (or as I do it, in the park.) We're more productive if we pull away from a situation and reflect. Which brings us naturally to the bedrock issues of long-term planning and goals.

Planning and Goals

The first year I homeschooled I had exactly 2 weeks notice! Week #1 was spent adjusting to the idea and finding books, and week #2 was spent on a family vacation with the books in tow. Even if you're short on time, give yourself two weeks to plan anyway. The time you spend ahead in preparation will reap results in productivity later.

- Planning ahead helps us to see the big picture for the school year.

- Knowing our unit choices ahead of time keeps us alert for help. Friends who have an interest in your topic of study will seem to pop up out of nowhere.

- Planning in the summer saves teaching time in the winter.

- Planning on paper reduces stress because our brains are not always trying to recall what it was we wantedto do.

- Supplies can be purchased ahead.

- Focusing on what's important is easier when we're not experiencing the tyranny of the urgent.

Someone has said, *"Choose to aim at nothing and you will hit the mark every time."* Why is orderly planning for life necessary? Because when there is no orderly planning for the use of your time, it's left to chance and chaos will soon reign. Personal fulfillment comes when you know you have spent your God-given time wisely in relation to the needs of your family, yourself, and outsiders.

You see, it really relieves the guilt when you look at the minutes you have in the day and you plan for the use of that time. At the end of the day, you look at the results and you honestly say, *"I did what I could with the time that I had."* We are humans who have needs for rest, exercise, nutritious food, solitude and time alone with God. When you plan for your day, don't overburden yourself with activity. Find the needed balance.

Rev. 9201

Advance with Regular Retreats
It's a good idea to set aside times for private planning. Start with a weekend away once a year with your spouse to pray and reflect. *"How are we doing? What are the goals for the coming year?"*

While you're at it, set aside other times for you to be alone with your husband and time for yourself alone. When Lee and I first began homeschooling, we committed ourselves to a weekly date night, just to talk. In times of plenty, a date night might include dinner in a restaurant. In lean times, date nights become more creative. Two eggrolls shared as we drive around the city looking at Christmas lights. A picnic beside the river. Watching movies on the big screen in my husband's office. (Yes, one Saturday night we bought Chinese-to-go and watched a borrowed family video in the office boardroom. The cleaning crew was shocked to find us there at that huge mahogany table dining by candlelight!)

Celebrate the good job you are doing homeschooling! It helps Mom, Dad, *and* the kids!

How to start
Prayerfully determine goals. Am I willing to give up my personal expectations and allow God, through a lifetime, to replace my goals with His? (Psalm 37, I Peter 3, I Cor. 2:9) Proverbs 3:6 says *"In all your ways acknowledge Him and He will establish your plans."*

As you think through goals, try to think of some tangible, measurable way to express them. For example, *"Susan will learn her times tables by Dec. 1."* or *"Adam will learn to rollerskate this year."* are two measureable goals. (See **Yearly** and **Monthly Goal Worksheets** in Appendix C.) If they're not measurable, how will you know when you've accomplished them?

After you seek goals through prayer, write them down so you can look back. *Write annual goals for yourself and your children on the yearly and monthly planning sheets.* You will then be able to see what sort of progress you are making, and initiate course corrections along the way.

Goals do not have to be elaborate. They can just be one or two things that God really impresses on you that are priorities this year. An example of a spiritual goal might be "our children will have a quiet time at least three mornings per week this semester." You may have a child who needs to learn telephone manners or table manners. You may be working on potty training or obedience with that two-year-old. Nothing's *too* practical!

"We've got these great goals... Now what?"

You've taken the time to develop goals prayerfully and written them out clearly. Now how do you set about accomplishing them?

1. *Determine how the goals will be accomplished.* Set short-term objectives. Decide how you will do what you plan to do.

2. *Schedule and plan your time.* Become an effective time manager. Manage the minutes.

3. *Set realistic objectives.* Don't say *"I'll teach the times tables in one week!"* Rather, say, *"I'll teach the 3's table or the 6's table in one week."* if that is more realistic for your child.

4. *Recognize your own personal limitations.* Plan less than you think you'll have time for — allow for the unexpected. You need sleep, time with your husband and quiet time with God. You can't do everything — Do what you have time to do.

5. *Be result oriented and not busy-work oriented.* Most workbooks you will find for the basics have more activity pages than you need (or want) to accomplish the results you're after. Publishers will tell you that you aren't expected to do every single page or every single follow-up activity recommended at the end of a reading story. Work towards goals you have chosen.

6. *Avoid slothfulness.* A sloth is an animal that hangs from a tree, eating the leaves from that trees where he hangs. He barely moves. He is so lazy that he sometimes won't even move after he has eaten all the leaves from the tree where he hangs. He would rather starve. Slothfulness is a powerful word. We really want to avoid laziness.

7. *Align yourself with a support group of like mind.* You will need the encouragement of your friends who are also home schooling. You will benefit from their enthusiasm, from their ideas, from their input. You will also benefit from having someone to call when things get hard.

8. *Seek the counsel of someone who can tell you if your curriculum is appropriate.* If you're a newcomer, unsure of yourself or have a child with special needs, please be sure to seek the counsel of someone who knows home school curriculum, who knows the nuts-and-bolts of home school teaching. Seek their counsel and listen to their advice.

Mom and Dad need to pray together and decide specific goals. Expect to do it annually. And do it individually for each child. Then, write out ways that you believe God is leading you to accomplish these goals.

Rev. 92011

Finally, if God tells you to homeschool — move forward, do it and don't look back. Don't look to the left or the right. Don't look at the new school that is being built one mile from your home or at the new equipment they are buying. Don't look at what other homeschooling Moms are accomplishing with their children. Look forward to the goals God has given *you*.

Covering All the Bases

People always ask, *"How do I know that I'm covering what I should in school?"* I try to simplify things by saying, *"Think 3-R's plus units."*

The 3 R's of course are "reading, writing, and 'rithmetic." Besides the 3-R's, you will do units of study. You will have spent on the average 90 minutes per day reading and writing and 45 minutes to one hour per day doing math. Unit studies will take an average of 1 1/2 hours per day (or, as mentioned before, some people do unit activities on one or two whole days per week and spend the rest of the days on academics). I'm only trying to let you see the balance, *not* give you times fixed in stone.

"Okay," you say to me, "even if I know what to cover, *how will I know that I did it?"* The answer? — Your school notebooks, especially those 3-ring binders for each child compiled throughout each school year. (Remember back a few pages ago?) By the end of the school year, each child's 3-ring binder will emerge as a portfolio highlighting his major accomplishments.

You don't want loose, flying papers. You don't want to emphasize worksheet, worksheet, worksheet. These don't have a place in the notebook. I'm not talking about keeping a loose-leaf binder with worksheets you did for the entire year. Samples are enough. I'm talking about recording information that is more valuable than that — something that will really represent your child's efforts, something that the child will look back on and be proud of. This binder will be something your youngster can hold in his hand and show Grandma and Grandpa when they come to visit at Christmas and ask, *"Well, what have you been learning this year?"*

And you can smile, knowing God's grace has turned plans and goals into reality!

Postscript to Planning for Success:

"Did God really say for me to homeschool?" That's a question I've asked myself more than one bleak February morning over the course of the last fifteen years.

I even remember one day, about ten years ago, when I found myself on the telephone calling local preschools to see if there were any sudden winter openings!` The person who detests daycare, the one who at that time was consulting approximately 50 families in the Richmond area about the benefits of homeschooling! But I had had it! I was ready to throw in the towel, say I was mistaken, that a human body could not withstand the pressures of homeschooling *and* being a homemaker!

Enter my level headed husband. *"You don't need a preschool,"* he said. *"You just need to see all that has and will continue to be accomplished! You need God's loving perspective!"* ("Yes," I thought, "I could use a few warm fuzzies right now, *and a Florida vacation wouldn't hurt, either!"*)

Throughout all of my personal struggles, I've come up with a few conclusions about *"How I Know I Am Doing What I Should"*:

First, I need to measure success by what I did, not by what I did not do. As a classroom teacher, I never accomplished all my hoped-for plans. As a mother, it is just as true. Life has its interruptions.
I must trust that God is in control of available time and look at the positive— what we *did* do!

God knows my frame — I am just clay. He has given us each 24 hours in the day. I am accountable only for what can be done humanly. *Do what you can with the time that you have!* How can we do that? *Allow God to speak the day's / week's / season's priorities and aim for them.*

As I write this, I have an eight-year-old whose basic reading and language skills are just about ready to take off. I am spending about 2 hours daily in one-on-one instruction with her because this is the "season" for it! That doesn't leave a lot of time for one-on-one with the other children. I'm not happy about it, but my 12-year-old is temporarily teaching herself math. As soon as I feel released from priority number one, I believe it will be time to go back with my older girl to pick up pieces in math with manipulatives and discussion with Mom. This type of teaching does not fit the class-room teaching mold, but it works well in homeschool.

For all the reasons we've discussed, it's important to develop specific goals. But even as you do, bring your old goals and expectations to the foot of the cross and place them on His altar as a sacrifice, knowing that He may replace them with something new and better and unexpected.

God is to be trusted: *"What eye has not seen and ear has not heard and has not entered into the heart of man, God has prepared for those who love Him."* As we release, He'll replace.

When life just refuses to follow your best-laid plans, let go and relax. Wait expectantly on Him — He will give you new goals and dreams. Prepare for the new thing He is going to do.

We must allow God to shoulder the responsibility for the results. He cares more for me and you than we will ever comprehend. The results matter to God. Remember — God has created us and our children with just the talents he intended. *He is pleased with His creation.* We are a promise!

When we began teaching our oldest daughter, Ashley, homeschooling was not a popular choice. As a matter of fact, most people thought we were making a dreadful mistake—one that would be costly for Ashley's future. Even I thought I was compromising academically. But Lee and I were convinced that character development mattered more to God than academic achievement. We were willing to make the sacrifice. Again, I underestimated God's total love for us. He had greater things, academically, planned for us than I could have ever dreamed. Our children's schooling has been rich. *Yours will be too!*

GOD IS TRAINING UP HIS HEROES, AND WHEN THEY APPEAR, THE WORLD WILL WONDER WHERE THEY CAME FROM. — C.S. LEWIS

Post-Postscript: Books that have helped me with Organization and Goals

Disciplines of a Beautiful Woman — Anne Ortlund

Sidetracked Home Executives — Pam Young & Peggy Jones

Is There Life After Housework? — Don Aslett

Do I Dust or Vacuum First? — Don Aslett

The Compleat Family Book — Elva Anson & Kathie Liden

Dinner's Ready — Mimi Wilson & Mary Beth Lagerborg

My First 300 Babies — Gladys Hendrick, Vision House

PRACTICAL TIPS

1. **Plan yearly/monthly goal sheets for yourself and your children.** *Plan the number of days you will attend school on the calendar. Check to see if your state has a minimum school day requirement.* Look at a calendar to see how you will space your units.

2. **Decide upon and write an appropriate daily/weekly schedule.** Remember, regularity is important and will produce brighter, happier, more productive children.

3. **Plan units to be studied ahead (in summer) on weekly unit planning sheets.** Save these in your school management notebook. Add anecdotal records to these pages at the end of the day or week.

4. **List and collect supplies you will be needing.** This will save time in the long run. Set up a central location for supplies near the area you will be using them. Plastic bins or labeled shoeboxes are handy for storing supplies.

5. **Use weekly assignment sheets for each reading child.** Use pencil to write daily lesson plans for these (you *will* need to erase from time to time.) Try to plan about one month's worth or one unit's worth of these at a time so you can check for a balance of choices.

6. **Weekly assignment sheets.** List assignments related to the basics and follow through related to the unit your family is studying. Remember that plans are meant to be changed. You can take longer to finish or carry a grammar workbook over to the next year. It is best to interrelate the vocabulary, reading assignments and writing as much as possible with the unit plans.

7. **Save samples in each child's 3-ring binder.**

8. **Review plans weekly. See if they are balanced.** And each evening, look over the next day's assignment to make needed adjustments.

9. **Start school on time each day after chores and breakfast.**

10. **Remember: You have 8-12 years to teach each child.** *Do what you can with the time that you have.*

11. **Compare yourself to no one.**

12. **Trust God for the results.**

Notes:

In this section...

- ## Teaching reading

- ## Cultivating and coaching young writers

- ## "What about grammar?"

Section Two
Language Arts
Taking the Mystery Out

It wasn't until I began to teach my own children at home that I discovered how simple it can all be.

When I began teaching in public schools straight out of college, I was totally unclear on what language arts really was. I was also very confused about the stages of reading development. It wasn't until I began to teach my own children at home and began to do research on my own that I discovered how simple it can all be. I hope this information will lift some of the burden that you may feel. Reading and writing are not only the foundation for everything else we accomplish, but they are also the most rewarding. Teach your child to read and it will be a joy both of you can remember for a lifetime!

When we speak of language arts, we are really speaking of just four basic processes: listening, speaking, reading, and writing. Listening begins at birth. The child listens to the sounds you make, imitates them and eventually this turns to speaking. In the typical school language arts curriculum, you'll find the following areas covered in language arts: reading, (including phonics instruction) and writing, which would include grammar, spelling, handwriting, and composition.

In the next two chapters, we'll strip away a lot of the unnecessary mystery (and worry) that surround teaching children reading and writing. In the next section, we'll build on that foundation to learn and explore and enjoy all the other disciplines.

Ready? Let's go!

In this chapter...

- ## Teaching beginning reading

- ## Stages of development

- ## Rediscovering the Classics

Section Two, Chapter One
Reading
— De-mystified

Teach your child to read. It will be a joy both of you can remember for a lifetime!

My purpose in this section is to clarify and simplify language arts — in particular reading. If you have an overview of the stages of reading from readiness through refined reading, an idea of what's included in each stage of reading and an idea of how to choose materials and activities, then you'll have a clear perspective when making plans for your child.

We've all heard the philosophy of homeschooling that says let the child bloom when he or she is ready and then he will learn rapidly.

It's axiomatic that a child must be developmentally ready for instruction. If he's not ready, he can't learn. Of course, we all agree with that. But don't let this lull you into thinking that all learning will occur naturally. It's important to use a systematic approach when teaching children to read.

Five stages of reading development
For example, there are stages of reading development and your child is in one of these stages right now. (As a matter of fact, so are you.) Your job is to commit yourself to a program of study appropriate to your child's needs. As a start, let's look at the stages of reading development and what to expect in each.

You may find these listed differently in other material, but basically the stages are the same. The first stage is *readiness*, next is *beginning reading*, then *rapid skill development*, followed by *wide reading*, and finally the *refinement stage* (which probably most of us are in.)

READING READINESS

It is important to develop your child's thinking capacity and vocabulary during this time. This will pay greater dividends in the future than early reading instruction.

However, don't be afraid to prepare your child to begin reading instruction during this preschool stage.

- **develop listening comprehension by reading aloud interesting non- fiction and quality literature**

- **use readiness workbooks with discretion**

- **put labels on chair, tent, doll, etc. Can your child find all the labels that start with /t/?**

- **display colorful pictures cut from magazines or done by the child with the title underneath**

- **use a bulletin board with weather report, messages, etc.**

- **write heading on pictures; write language experience stories**

- **practice listening and speaking extensively**

- **combine learning activities with play or games**

- **make alphabet books (teach the sound of the letter, NOT just the name of the letter)**

- **recognize the alphabet, begin printing letters**

- **read road signs, labels**

- **recognize short words in stories; listen to story records**

- **learn to print name, using lower case letters after the first letter of name**

- **teach the left to right process of reading**

- **begin to distinguish among letter forms and sounds**

- **begin to tell whether two words begin with the same letter**

- **listen to a word and supply 2-3 words that begin with the same sound; supply rhyming words**

- **note similarities and differences in word endings, middles, and beginnings.**

Reading Readiness

Before jumping into letter sounds and flashcards, think first of developing both a strong vocabulary base for your child and a broad foundation of experiences and information.

Children need to think and do. Let your pre-schooler have as many experiences as possible outside of what we would consider formal reading instruction. Expose him to lots of different activities — a visit to the fire station, to the zoo, to the rescue squad - all the usual field trips that pre-schoolers take, imparting as much information as you can along the way.

Not only does he learn the word car, but he learns the name for that car or the particular parts of the car—the accelerator, the engine, the ignition. Pass along your adult vocabulary and wealth of information.

A wealth of experiences will benefit your young child even more than early instruction in phonics. These experiences prepare him to read for information and understanding later in grade school. So, whatever you know, pass it on. I guarantee you that your experience and vocabulary are more extensive than your preschooler's.

There are several ways to start readiness instruction with your child. One is to develop listening comprehension by reading, reading, reading to them. Read lots of non-fiction. Not just pre-school style books. Include books on a much higher level. Interpret what you read to your child. Discuss the pictures. Your child will be learning.

Use quality literature. We discovered by accident how much our preschool aged children learn by the trickle-down effect— that is by being around while the older children and I read and discuss high interest books.

Read-aloud books such as Dr. Seuss and nursery rhymes develop your child's ear for sounds, too.

Eventually, you will do more and more with your child to help him distinguish between particular letter sounds. For example, try "I am going to say three words to you. *Car / hat / hop.* Which two words begin with the same sound?" Both of you can enjoy little activities like that. And if he hears the two sounds that are the same, let him jump two times. Incorporate movement in the activity. Children like it better and stay interested longer.

Car time works well for readiness games. As you drive along, have your child supply rhyming words. *"Let's see how many words we can say to rhyme with cat: cat, bat, sat, mat, etc."* (An advance visit with Dr. Seuss may help Mom with this.)

Make an alphabet book together. If your child enjoys cutting and pasting, take one page for each letter of the alphabet and put pictures on the page of items that begin with that letter. You might have a picture of a banana and a ball and a bat on the 'B' page.

We've all heard of the system of putting labels on things around the house—the chair, the doll, the bed. If you do this, the child won't stay interested in the labels for more than a day or two. The labels just become a part of his environment that he doesn't even notice. But the label game is fun while it lasts.

For example, with the label on the refrigerator, you might say, *"I think there is something in this room that starts with the sound (r). I wonder what it is. Do you think you could find it?"* When your child finds that the refrigerator begins with that sound, you could have him point to the "r" . Pretty soon, he begins to associate the beginning sound with the letter "r". You haven't even mentioned that the letter is called "R". You are dealing with the letter sound, not the letter name.

Display your child's drawing and have the child give you a sentence about the picture you can write underneath. That gives your child not only the idea of writing, but of reading for information. Read and re-read the label for each family member.

Try language experience stories. For this, your child simply dictates a story to you which you write out. Then you read the story back to him. You can expand on the fun, too Have the child find a certain familiar word that is repeated in the story, or find words that begin with a particular sound. "Find the word that begins with 'T'."

Do what your youngster is *ready* to do. He may just be ready to dictate a sentence to you. Read it back to him and have him draw a picture to go with the story.

Language experience is a great tool for reading readiness. Be creative with it. You want your child to practice listening and speaking extensively. Listen to your child when he or she relates an event or story to you. That gives him practice in speaking. Give your child chances to listen to oral storytelling, or to tapes, or to books read to him.

Storybook cassettes are good for your pre-reader. Record some of these so that the child can listen to the same story over and over. When he listens to the record, help him turn the page at the correct time to get the idea of the words on the page, the left to right flow, and the sequence of turning pages.

Children who listen to the same story over and over, often begin to recognize particular words in the story. They might even point to a child's name in the story and say, *"Oh, I know! —that says Sam."* This is a sign of visual readiness for reading. He can remember the shapes of words!

Some pre-schoolers are ready for reading flashcards. Young children who are strong visual learners will often begin to recognize words by their shape. Many homeschooled children this age are learning phoneme (letter) sounds and simple sight vocabulary. (By the way, youngsters often begin to read road signs or McDonald's signs because they recognize the symbols. Teach the child the meanings of those signs.)

In this stage, it's always best to combine whatever activity you choose with a game. Children in this stage respond much more readily to games than to formal instruction. That's why I suggested you make games out of the labels in your kitchen. But make games of other things, too.

Maybe you could have your little one look through the story he dictated to see how many G's he can find, while you hunt for S's. The person who finds the most wins the contest with an M&M as the prize. Who could resist such a fun game!?

Go along with your child's interests. If it's fun for both you and the child, make flashcards and begin to build a sight reading vocabulary. When he becomes restless, stop the activity. Try it another time or another way later. Later, when the child is ready, you will teach the system of our language—*phonics.*

READINESS FOR PHONICS

Language experience is a necessary prerequisite. Your child is experiencing language when he talks, describes, re-tells an event, dictates stories or letters.

Develop adequate auditory and visual discrimination:

auditory -
— hear sounds at the beginning, middle, and end of words
— rhyming words

visual - mark letter or word that is same or different.

accurate, distinct speech - vowels, lisps, dialect (/*pin*/vs. /*pen*/)

Readiness for Phonics

How do you know when your child is ready for phonics instruction? Let me give you a few clues.

Has your child had an abundance of exposure to language? Has your child had plenty of opportunity for telling you events, stories, describing things he has seen? Has he had plenty of opportunity to retell a sequence of events or to dictate stories to you?

(By the way, encourage your preschooler to speak accurately, clearly, and distinctly. If he has a lisp, try to encourage him to speak clearly and say the letters accurately. If your child has a dialect as we do in our area of the country and maybe says *"tint"* instead of *"tent"* with a short /e/ then work on this, first with your-self and then with your child. The more accurately the child speaks, the more easily he learns phonics.)

Has he had opportunity to recognize any of the beginning letter sounds? Check whether he has adequate auditory and visual discrimination to be able to understand phonics instruction.

If your child can hear sounds at the beginning and the end of words, that's a clue he is ready for beginning phonics. Can your child supply rhyming words in some of the games that you have been playing? These two flags signal auditory readiness.

Can your child listen to a word and then give the same beginning sound? For example, if you gave the word *"first"*, he might say *"fist"* or *"fall"*. Can your child determine whether two words rhyme? For example, if you say *"cat"* and *"car"*, does he think those two words rhyme? These are things that you can not only observe but be working on.

Visually, if a child can mark a letter that is the same or different, he is discriminating letter shapes. For example, if you write a capital "A" and then in a row you list a small "a", an "A" written sideways, and an "A" written exactly as the capital "A" you wrote, and maybe a "B", can your child select the letter which is exactly the same as the letter that you wrote? That is a clue to whether a child is visually ready for phonics instruction.

Can your child actually see differences in letters printed side by side? He will need to do this to receive phonics instruction.

(Of course, you may ask *"What about 'B's and 'D's?"* since it's not uncommon for a child to reverse B's and D's even as late as age 8 or 9. Those letters are quite similar. We're looking for the more obvious in the readiness stage.)

Beginning Reading Instruction

All children learn school subjects with three modalities: visual, auditory, kinesthetic/tactile. Some are stronger visually, others auditorily or kinesthetically. (Remember *Individual Learning Differences* in *Why Home School?*) Each child is a unique individual. Here are three examples, all from the same family.

Beth: Strong visual learner. Learned to read in six weeks, at age 7. No formal reading instruction before that time, except that she knew the sounds of the letters. Entirely resistant to learning to read before the age of 7.

Learned with an eclectic approach: sight word cards, memorizing shapes of words, lots of dictation and copying exercises, some incidental phonics instruction. Was taught intensive phonics *after* she was a reader (again picked this up in about 6 weeks of intensive instruction.) Motivation for learning to read? Peer pressure, desire to read funny books like **Amelia Bedelia**, love of words and language.

This child will be a "star" student. Schoolteachers love her because she is so "teachable".

Debra: Strong kinesthetic learner. Loves to move, be outdoors, preferably running; loves handiwork, crafts, but not drawing; did not like to listen to stories as a toddler, wouldn't sit still for books, easily distracted.

Learning to read was a slow painful process, many reversals, trouble remembering sequence of letters, weak visual memory. Was taught to read using kinesthetic approach: letters in sand, in large print on blackboard, games that involved large body movement to hold interest. This child had to learn perseverance. Then, between 9 and 10, hit that spot where developmentally ready to read.

The end result? By age ten, this child was an excellent reader with extremely good concentration skills. This "straight-A" student can study for hours and will methodically attack any task, no matter how difficult. Spelling is still a real problem. As an adult, she will probably have to use the spell check on the computer.

Deep spiritual side. Thinks with the right side of her brain. Non-verbal, loves animals, sensitive. Communicates easily with God in prayer. This child will probably be in mercy ministries one day.

Steve: Strength—auditory. Would rather talk than learn to read. Loves people and friends. Loves to listen to a tape or have someone read to him. People are more important than books. He would do well in school if he could just concentrate and not think about playing with friends.

Interesting point: He was able to read the Bible fluently before any other book. Does this have something to do with having heard the Bible read for years before beginning to read on his own?

Vocalizes when sounding out difficult words. Taped books are okay but he won't look at the words if he can help it so Mom still needs to be nearby.

Learned to read in three years. Systematic phonics with all other suggestions used.

Motivation: *"You can see the movie when you read the book."*

Sing the words (ex. hymns) to learn to read.

This child may grow up to be leader of the men's fellowship.

The best way to teach all children is to use all three senses when you are instructing. In phonics instruction, the child will *hear* distinct differences in letter sounds and you will emphasize clarity. He will *see* distinct shapes and you will use flashcards to reinforce visually. He will take letters / words / sentences from dictation either on paper or on a large surface such as the blackboard or in a tray of sand. (*kinesthetic / tactile*). Use all three senses when you teach a child to read.

Teach new information to his strengths, but also use variety. A strong visual learner will learn quickly from flashcards while a strong kinesthetic learner will respond better to games that involve large motor movement to learn new information, but train *all* of the senses. All children have capabilities in all three areas. Why waste part of a brain when you're instructing?

"Catching on to the System"
Beginning reading instruction usually starts in kindergarten, though it's not a good idea to attach ages to any stage of reading.

Using a systematic structured approach to teaching phonics is important. When your child was younger, you might have taught some words by their shape (sight) (This works with strong visual learners.) Those children might even come to this stage with a visual reading vocabulary. Other children may come to this point knowing no words.

Either way, *our point is to teach the system of our language—how to break the code or "decode".* You want your child to know the system of our language. A child who does not learn this may have trouble by third or fourth grade when he begins to try to figure out longer 3 or 4 syllable words like "indivisible" or "incorporation." The first step in breaking the code of of language is understanding that we have *consonants* and *vowels*. You don't need to use those words yet—just help them see that different sounds blend together to make words.

Start beginning reading instruction by teaching the alphabet sounds. Not the names. Not how to recite the alphabet. Begin with a few consonants, then add one or two vowels to teach the sounds of letters. If your child seems interested, once he or she picks up two or three consonant sounds and even one vowel sound, you can begin to blend these sounds together.

For example, let your child choose two consonants from his own name. Talk about the sounds of those letters. If, for example, one of the consonants was H and another was T, you would teach the child the /h/ sound (*h*op) and the /t/ sound (ba*t*). Perhaps another letter in his name is A. Teach the /a/ sound (h*a*t).

Just by knowing those three letter sounds, your child can begin to blend. You can show your child how the /h/ and the /a/ blend to make /ha/, and if you add a /t/, you have the word "*hat*". Almost as soon as you've taught a few consonants and one or two vowels, you begin blending these sounds so that your child sees the system. Once your child sees the system, he will begin putting together sounds with your reinforcement.

Start blending as soon as possible. Suppose you get to that blending stage and it just doesn't click? The child just doesn't understand; it is like a foreign language to him. Well, that's a clue that you need to stop. Change direction for a while. Emphasize vocabulary development, thinking skills, language experience, and reading aloud. Come back in a few weeks to see if there is more interest. Make it a game and vary your style of presentation.

How long *"catching on to the system"* takes varies from child to child. Some might catch on immediately while others might need longer to see the system. Use lots of variety and practice for this to happen. Vary your style of presentation: use the chalkboard, markers, a large pan of rice to write in, chocolate pudding to write in with the finger, magnetic letters, etc. to make this a fun game of learning letter sounds and blends.

When a child has trouble with a word, try saying the word and then pronouncing it slowly enough to hear the individual sounds. If he doesn't seem to be really looking and paying attention to the letters in the word have him spell the word aloud to notice the letters .

Eventually, it will become easier to just teach words and let the child discover rules for those words rather than teaching a rule for every single pattern. In this beginning stage of reading, you don't have to worry about that. You won't have to teach every phonics rule known to man. That does not mean that you will not analyze words with your child to discover why certain words sound certain ways, but you won't need to teach your child a list of 90 rules to memorize for phonics. His reading will take off long before that point.

The key to success here is *consistent repetition* on a *daily basis* over a period of time. Short daily doses of instruction (10-15 minutes) are much better than long lessons once or twice a week.

Choose interesting reading material that does not present an excessive word recognition problem. This might be challenging. A curriculum you choose might not give enough practice reading material. Buy, borrow, or create your own practice readers to supplement your phonics instruction program.

Each day include an element of writing in your phonics instruc-tion. At first, the child may just write letters or simple words. If his motor skills are not developed enough to use a pencil, have him use magnetic letters or letter cubes to practice writing words.

Later, the child may copy or write simple phrases/sentences such as "The cat sat.", etc. Choose easy sentences from his readers for dictation.

WHY TEACH PHONICS?

Our language is 90% regular —
in other words, a letter or combination of letters
make predictable sounds in words.

Possible trouble during middle grades without it.

There are fewer phonetic sounds to recall than there are words
in our language. No one wants to memorize all the words in our
language by sight.

Spelling is easier when you know the phonics rules.

Phonics is systematic.

Maintain a balanced approach to reading instruction.
Spend only a short period each day on phonics.
Rules should not be drilled at the expense of real reading time.

Why Phonics?

By this point you may question "Why all this emphasis on phonics?" (Not to worry — others do too.) There are several reasons why phonics is an essential ingredient in reading instruction.

First of all, our language is 90% regular. (We often notice the *ir*regularities, but analysis shows our language is more than 90% regular.) You can see that if a child has had adequate phonics instruction, he or she should be able to attack practically any word he meets.

A youngster may have trouble during the middle grades if he did not receive phonics as part of his beginning reading instruction. A child taught to read by sight only in the early grades may seem to have no trouble in those beginning years of school. When he reaches words such as "migration", "theoretical" or "constitutionality" in grade 3 or 4 though, he has no clue how to decipher words if he has never been taught the system of our language.

Phonetic sounds are more easily recalled than sight words. Learning a list of 3000 sight words by rote memory is a mind-numbing challenge, but if the child has phonetic tools, he can analyze almost any word, whether or not he has seen it.

Most children's spelling will be better if they know the phonics rules. (The exception is children whose weakest modality is visual. Weak visual learners have difficulty remembering how words look and so may spell phonetically but not always correctly.) Why? Again because of the 90% regularity of our language. If a child knows the phonics rules, he should be able to spell nearly 90% of the words in our language. (Nearly 90% because spelling is not just phonics but also recalling the looks of what we have read.)

Phonics is systematic, methodical. It is acting in a prearranged, orderly way (the opposite of a hit or miss program.) Phonics gives a logical, orderly approach to learning to read. The child will learn that words are composed of parts which are sounded together. Is it an accident that language has patterns? If we think of the character of God, isn't he orderly and systematic? Look at the world He has created. It just seems logical that whenever we can point out the patterns and give a system to our children, we are choosing God's way to do things.

It will take a little longer to teach reading with phonics than with the sight word approach. (At least it will seem like it is taking longer in the beginning.) If you stick with it though, your child will catch up quickly once he gains phonic awareness and progress more rapidly than if he had been taught with a strictly sight word approach.

TEACHING BEGINNING READING

1. Consonant Sounds — being sure not to add a vowel when pronouncing the consonant

2. Vowel Sounds — short vowels first

3. Blending Sounds — /pa/ /t/ not /p/ /a/ /t/. You do not need to wait until you have taught all the consonant and vowel sounds before you begin blending. Blend as soon as your child catches on.

4. When a child has trouble with the word, pronounce the whole word first and then slowly to hear individual sounds. You may have the child "sound" spell the word to "notice" letters and pronounce.

5. Read interesting material that does not present an excessive word recognition problem. Three errors per page should be maximum!

6. Basal readers (readers with controlled vocabulary): Words are introduced only after the child has received sufficient instruction to attack them. (These words are used again and again in the readers.)

7. Read aloud a passage so that your child can hear "fluency". Then have him read the same passage back to you.

8. Do simultaneous oral reading with your child.

9. Include a writing component every day.

Curriculum Choices for Beginning Reading

If you're like most of us, when you start looking at the 100 plus beginning reading approaches available, your head starts swimming. How can you possibly choose the best? How much should you spend?

First of all, know that there is no perfect reading curriculum. A curriculum is a tool in the hands of a teacher — like a hammer in the hands of a carpenter. You will use the product; it will not teach your child. The average homeschool Mom goes through three beginning reading curriculums before finding her favorite (usually the third one.) My advice? Relax and browse around until you find a tool you feel comfortable with and will use consistently.

Secondly, price is not always an indication of the value of a reading curriculum. You can choose a volkswagen or a cadillac and they will both get you where you are going. The difference?

A volkswagen approach to beginning reading instruction is what I call the bare bones approach. *"Just the facts, ma'am. Nothing more."* A volkswagen will get you where you are going, though the ride might not be as comfortable as in a cadillac.

What does a volkswagen reading curriculum have? The rules. Words and short sentences or paragraphs to accompany the rules. Very simple instructions to teach the rules. No color. Not a lot of fluff. To this, you add your own flashcards, separately purchased workbooks and easy readers, boardwork, dictation, and your own good ideas when they come. A volkswagen is very inexpensive, even when you add the cost of separately purchased workbooks because there are excellent systematic workbooks and readers on the market at a low price.

A cadillac lets you ride in style. You'll get the rules, colorful workbooks, flashcards, and readers. You might even get tapes and games you don't have to invent.

You are probably thinking of investing in a cadillac because you don't want to have to think—*"Just give me everything I need"* you say. *Sorry, ma'am.* A curriculum that can read your child's mind has not and will never be written. You alone are your child's teacher. A curriculum is a tool.

More bad news — there is no curriculum on the market that you won't have to change and adapt. In some places, the workbooks will seem to move too fast or too slow. The tapes will seem to work for awhile and then learning seems to stop. Is this the curriculum's fault? Probably not. All engines need a tune-up from the master mechanic now and then. You'll need to make adjustments to any curriculum you purchase.

So what tool should you buy? Again, buy one you are comfortable with and will use consistently. The cadillac will include more options—a luxury for some. A volkswagen will give you the basics—the system of our language—the rules, word lists, short sentences or stories, and probably no color. The cadillac will give you the system plus extras: colorful readers, workbooks, audio tapes, maybe even games.

Invest wisely. Extra dollars may make the ride more comfortable but both will get you to your destination. Either way, there will be maintenance checkups along the route.

In my homeschool travels, I've met dozens of homeschooling moms who've taught their children to read on a shoestring budget. You can do it too, if you like. Then again, perhaps you'd enjoy the luxury of a cadillac...

Thirdly, be aware that there are significant differences in approach. Some programs emphasize rhyming word families such as *"hat, cat, sat, bat."* (Having the child change the initial consonant but noticing the same ending sound.) Other curriculums concentrate on blending the first two letters of the word from left to right. (For example, the "c "and the "a" blend to make *"cat"* or the "c" and the "a" blend to make *"cap"*.) This is important because ours is a left to right system of reading and writing. Rhyming word families are fine for occassional drill, but we should teach our children to blend from left to right. Keep this in mind when selecting curriculum.

No matter what your choice, remember that the home is the best place for diagnostic/prescriptive teaching. When your friends ask *"What approach are you using to teach your child at home?"* simply respond, *"I'm using a diagnostic/prescriptive approach"* and they won't ask you any more questions.

Just in case they do, "diagnostic/prescriptive" simply means that you see what the child knows (or doesn't know) and you prescribe or plan a lesson for the next day which will teach him what he needs to learn. You assess the situation (*diagnosing* the problem), and you write a *prescription* for it. You decide what to do next to teach unlearned skills.

No curriculum knows your child as well as you do!
You are the one who can make the best choices for your child, especially regarding any particular day's instruction. Diagnostic/ prescriptive teaching is best done in the home. In fact, there is no better place for it. Another word for it is tutoring. You are meeting your child's individual needs daily. Assessing a situation, seeing what his weaknesses and strengths are, and planning your next day's lessons based on what you know about your own child.

You will always be making choices to delete or add steps to any program. If a child has mastered a concept, why have him repeat 10 worksheets on that concept? If a child does not understand, you create a new way to present the information until he does understand and you can move on.

Your curriculum is only a tool to accomplish the work you have set out to do. That tool does not need to be expensive, either. A volkswagen and a cadillac will both get you where you're going.

COMPONENTS OF A READING PROGRAM:

1. **The rules ("Just the facts, ma'am.")**

2. **Readers (teacher made or bought) using controlled vocabulary**

3. **Follow up practice**
   (workbooks, sentences written on blackboard)

4. **Flashcards (pictures do not teach the child to read, by the way)**

5. **Dictation (sounds, words, sentences)**

6. **Listening and interacting with Mom**
   (*"How would you end this story?"*
   ***Would you like for me to read you this great book?"*)**

Staying out of the pit

A common pitfall in any heavily phonetic reading program is that you come out with a child who reads in a slow, labored manner, letter sound by letter sound, rather than blending. Encourage your child to read words as a whole rather than in parts. Read the word list or story to the child so he can hear the way it should sound. Occasionally use sight readers to encourage whole word reading and pull your child out of the letter by letter habit of reading. This will help your child get the ideas: *words should flow* and *we read for meaning*.

To stay out of the pit, be sure to add the following three elements to any beginning phonics program you use: language experience, dictation, and flashcards.

What is "language experience"? For beginning readers it is simply a carryover from their experiences as pre-readers — speaking, listening, seeing. For example, just as with a pre-schooler, you could let your child dictate a story or experience for you to write out. (Then use that story for teaching.) Add lots of language experience to your phonics program.

Also, add daily writing to any phonics program you use. This can be as simple as copying words or sentences. It can be writing blends or words from dictation. Write each day.

Finally, don't overlook the benefit of flashcards. They help build fluency in reading. Use them isolated or build sentences with them. Introduce flashcards of new words before presenting a new easy phonetic reader, always connecting the system of our language (phonics) with the visual shape of the word.

Reading—The Whole Picture

To focus on phonics only would be like telling you all the benefits of eating protein and ignoring vegetables, grains, and fruits. Beginning readers should receive a daily dose of intensive phonics instruction, but phonics is not the only thing you use to teach your child to read. It may be the core of your beginning reading instruction program, but there is more.

Understanding phonics is like having a tool. This tool will be used by the child for lifelong learning. The whole object of reading is to be able to use that ability to learn. We are sharpening and forging that phonics instrument to be used by the child all his life in order to facilitate learning. We know that reading is much more than phonics and can't be isolated from the rest of life. Ours is a connected learning approach. All disciplines are related.

Don't overlook reading for understanding. Of course your child will have that perspective of reading because you will be reading aloud together for enjoyment frequently from books that provide information that you both try to understand together.

No one knows how a human being really learns to read. Probably no two people learn in exactly the same way. We are too complex for that. Language is a gift to mankind from our Creator. He has given all of us the ability to communicate with words. Your child *will* learn to read!

SAMPLE — A WEEK OF EASY READER LESSONS

A beginning reader instruction approach. Obviously, this cannot be done for every single story, but it is good to take one passage per week and teach it thoroughly. Remember the Homeschool Motto: QUANTITY AND PAPER PRODUCTION ARE NOT SO IMPORTANT AS DOING SOMETHING THOROUGHLY. The beginning reader will learn more from the repetition and ease of this approach than he will by having new stories introduced every day.

Monday— Read the story aloud to the child. Let him hear fluency modelled by you and let him enjoy the story. Teach the child unknown words. Use flashcards. You read the words. Explain the phonic sounds. Then have the child read them.

Tuesday— Review and reteach flashcards, emphasizing decoding of the words. Have the child read the story simultaneously with you. Then have the child read aloud to you. Use the flashcards to make sentences. Give a mixed up group of the flashcards and have the child arrange a sentence. Make funny sentences, too. Encourage the child to re-read this story silently several times over the next 3-4 days.

Wednesday— Review again, the flashcards from the story. Have the child read the story silently alone and then aloud to you or a family member.

Thursday— Have child copy words or sentences from the story. (Children who do not have the motor skills to copy may use letter cubes.) Review flashcards.

Friday— Have child take words/sentences from dictation.

RAPID READING DEVELOPMENT

During the rapid skill development stage, your child, who has learned the basic word attack skills, will develop fluency and ease in reading. Allow him to read a wide variety of very easy books and by the end of this stage he will most likely be able to read skillfully, attacking almost any unfamiliar word.

- **Don't kill the desire to read with too much drill and exercise - Use basal readers and teacher's guides with discretion.**

- **Average time spent on daily instruction and assignments in reading is between 60-90 minutes. Decide how to balance your time among these! (Base your decisions on your goals.)**

  - **reading**

  - **literature (read aloud by *you*!)**

  - **handwriting**

  - **phonics**

  - **spelling**

  - **creative writing**

  - **dictation**

  - **grammar (optional at this stage)**

- **Don't neglect oral reading — both by you and the child. Oral reading provides practice in communication skills and aids effective speech patterns.**

Rapid Development of Skills

Your child has learned the basic word attack skills and now needs to develop fluency and ease in reading. Encourage him to read a wide variety of very easy books. If you allow him to do this, by the end of this stage he will most likely be able to read skillfully, attacking almost any unfamiliar word.

Most of us tend to push our children into books we think are more meaningful (that is, *harder*.) But allow your child plenty of time to develop fluency by reading the easiest books he can find.

Encourage him to read for fun. Don't kill his desire to read with too much drill and exercise. (A *short* daily period is plenty.) Use basal readers and teacher's guides with discretion since all teacher's guides have more material than you are truly expected to cover.

Most homeschoolers average 60-90 minutes in daily instruction and assignment time at this stage of reading. Remember all the things included in language arts — reading instruction, reading aloud "great books", handwriting, spelling, composition, grammar — and decide how to best divide your time among these areas.

Each subject doesn't need to be covered each day. In fact, there are "seasons" for some subjects — such as grammar. Most of us have grand illusions of accomplishment during a school year, buying too many workbooks to finish. We don't have the time to use everything we purchase or everything we see that is good. Pick and choose according to the goals you have set for this period of time. Don't feel obligated to teach every facet of language arts every day!

Your child is probably now an accomplished "silent reader". But have him continue to read orally to you often. This will provide practice in communication skills and will help your child's speech patterns. He may not want to read aloud to you. But that doesn't mean you don't do it. (Reading to little brother or sister may provide another outlet.) You want to develop children who can read both silently and orally.

In choosing resources for this stage, some of you will choose a safe, prepared curriculum by nationally recognized publishers. Balance the suggestions in the teacher's manuals with your own common sense. Don't feel compelled to do every idea that is suggested. Be sure the reading program does not consume you so that you lose sight of your goals.

Remember, being goal oriented saves you time and gets you to the point. Your child becomes a fluent reader so that he can learn. A reading instruction program should be used to get him to the point of fluency so that he can get on with learning.

GOALS FOR RAPID READING DEVELOPMENT

- the child will read smoothly with the ability to attack almost any unfamiliar word.

- He will read silently with understanding at a rate equal to or faster than orally.

- He will read for pleasure.

- He will read for facts in a textbook and will know how to go to non-fiction resources for information.

If your program is taking so long to finish that you have no time left for exploration, discovery, and real learning, then you are working towards a burnt out child and mother.

Some home teachers forego the basal reader approach and instead depend on easy readers from the library or other sources. Look for readers that introduce only a few new words at a time.

Evaluate your child's understanding with questioning and discussion after he has read a passage. Pay attention to what he tells you, and you'll know if he understood what he read. That's comprehension: whether he understands what he reads.

When selecting easy readers, remember that research has shown that the easier a reader is for a child, the more progress that child will tend to make. (Who needs research to figure *that* out, right?) In one study, the best average gains were made by children who made fewer than 3 errors per 100 words. Check the readability of material for your child by counting off approximately 100 words and having the child read that section to you. If he makes fewer than 3 errors, you know you have chosen an appropriate book.

Don't put your child in reading material that is too difficult because you think he needs pushing. If you do, you will push your child into the frustration level and learning will actually slow down or stop. (It was also noted in the same research that the easier the reader, the better the child's behavior. Is *that* a surprise to any of us?)

As a fourth and fifth grade teacher, I noticed that each year I would have children in my class who were just approaching this rapid skill development stage. It often takes that much time to grasp the system of our language, and they had not yet developed fluency. Yet in the fourth grade, children in schools are traditionally introduced to textbooks which introduce many new vocabulary words on one page. This is quite a challenge to a child who is not yet fluent. That child cannot understand what he reads because he is still reading so slowly that he loses the meaning of a passage with too many new words.

Allow your child to work through this stage, no matter how old he is. *Give him the luxury of the time to read, read, read to build fluency.* What he is reading is not as important as the fact that he is reading.

WIDE READING

During the wide reading stage of development, which usually occurs in the second half of elementary school, there will be less emphasis on the development of reading ability and more emphasis on functional and recreational reading. As new words are met, meaning, rather than simply pronunciation will be important.

- **Review phonics.**

- **If necessary, teach syllabification.**

- **Teach use of dictionary.**

- **Do lots of silent reading (daily) without neglecting oral reading.**

- **Check on comprehension with questions, discussions; include understanding the central idea of a paragraph, the feelings of a character or anticipating what will happen next.**

- **Teach how to locate, summarize, and organize information.**

- **Have the child read good literature and non-fiction books that pertain to subject areas being studied.**

Wide reading

This stage usually occurs in the second half of elementary school. Now there is less focus on the decoding skills and more emphasis on reading for recreation or for a purpose. The child not only reads just to pronounce words, but he learns that he must read for understanding and meaning.

During this stage, integrate reading assignments with the subjects you are studying. For example, if you are studying explorers, you may have your child read an interesting biography of Magellan or DeSota or Columbus. Notice I said nothing about buying a "reading book" from a publisher? If you are doing enough reading related to the units you are studying, *you won't have time for basal readers*. This is much more effective than taking isolated, short reading passages from a reading book which pertain to nothing else in the child's life. The best approach to learning is always integrated.

Review phonics rules as needed. Observe the types of errors your child is making when reading or writing and reteach rules as needed. Teach your child to divide words into syllables (syllabification) in order to decode them. Teach him to use the dictionary. Teach your child how to scrutinize textbooks, and how to locate, organize and summarize information. (You'll teach your child a lot of this as you go to the library for reference work together.) Have your child read good literature and good non-fiction books.

Comprehension Skills

During the wide reading stage, you will begin to think more about developing comprehension skills and vocabulary with your child. Note that comprehension is simply understanding — nothing more. During the wide reading stage, understanding is reading.

We've passed the stage of decoding and now the child knows that the purpose of learning to read is to read for meaning.

We'll look at specific aspects of comprehension shortly, but keep in mind that comprehension is not something that can be dissected and taught part by part. Our children are not machines, they are humans. It is much more effective to think of comprehension as understanding.

All aspects of comprehension are related. If your child, for example, can read for the main idea, he can probably also read for details and answers to questions. He can probably grasp the author's plan and read critically, not swallowing everything he sees in print. Let's take a closer look at what we're after.

First of all, your child should be able to read for the main idea. The reader gets to *the main idea* by following the author's smaller guideposts— the main idea of each paragraph, each caption, each section, each chapter along the way. You can gauge your youngster's grasp by asking:

• *What feelings did the main character have?*
• Give me a one sentence summary of the incident.
• Select the main idea of each paragraph.
• What is the topic sentence of this paragraph?
• Write headlines and a title for this selection.
• Why did the author include this caption..., this headline, etc.?
• *Tell me about the introduction and conclusion of this selection.*

You won't need to use all of these suggestions each time. Vary them as appropriate. If your child understands what he reads he will not only get the main idea, but be able to communicate it.

Your child should learn to skim to get the total impression of a piece before reading it. You skim when you pick up a news magazine. Teach your child to glance through material before jumping in.

Your child may learn to read for details or answers to specific questions. If this is your plan, give him questions before he sits down to read a passage so he can think about them as he reads.

Your child may read for the sequence of events and be able to re-tell this to you. If that's your intent, tell the child before he starts reading.

He should be able to understand printed directions. If not, there's a problem that will show up in other areas. Does your child have trouble understanding what he reads? If so, perhaps he really doesn't belong in wide reading materials yet. He may still need to read books that will build fluency. Until he's ready, you can read books aloud to him that have content he needs to understand.

Over time (usually around age twelve) your child will develop the ability to understand the author's plan. Was the author's intention to persuade you to his point of view? or was it to inform? What was his purpose? *"Why does this author write as he does?"*

As your child matures, you will want him to read more critically. For example, he may compare two authors that contradict each other. Let's think again about reading that biography of Magellan. If your child reads two biographies of Magellan, he may find conflicting evidence in the two books. Which is truth? How can we judge? Just because something is printed does not mean it is always true. Recognizing that is learning to think critically.

Encourage your youngster to consider new information in light of what he already knows. After reading the two biographies of Magellan, help him analyze the truth of what he has read based on what he already knows. Show your child how *you* would read for meaning. How would you review the content of a chapter?

He should be able to read creatively. For example, have him stop before the end of a passage and think of his own ending. What would happen if...? This is something you can also do when you are reading aloud with your child. Stop in the middle of a chapter and say, *"What do you think will happen next? What do you think she will decide to do?"*

While it is important to continue occasional oral reading, your child will now do a lot of silent reading because he is a fluent reader. By now, you can depend on his ability to read silently, but how will you check comprehension?

Have you ever had a friend go to a movie and come back excitedly wanting to tell you all about it? If you're really interested, you'll ask questions: *"Well, why did he choose to do that? What happened next?... No, don't tell me the end, I might want to go see it myself."*

If you do the same sort of thing with your child after he has read a book, you will know whether he understands the central idea of that paragraph or story or book by what he tells you. If you find that he didn't really understand what he read, then go back and read with him. Help him to analyze and understand. You might also make a mental note that perhaps the book is too difficult for him and you will choose an easier one next time.

Also, you don't want your child to always read for literal information. *You want your child to begin to make judgments and inferences about he reads.*

Please don't take this too seriously and think, *"Oh no, I can't do this."* Inference simply means seeing beyond the facts. *We sometimes call this "reading between the lines" — whether we are literally reading or not!* We all make inferences everyday. Since you are an adult and you think like an adult, when you read material aloud with your child, you will naturally see more than the surface detail. Simply discuss what's happening that's not spelled out in the text. (*"Who do you think ate the cookie?"*) Your child will naturally learn to make inferences and judgments beyond word for word content of the story. In fact, you'll be surprised at what they come up with!

REDISCOVER THE CLASSICS

WHY STUDY THE CLASSICS? You can use good literature as an instrument in building Christian character and a love of learning in your children!

SUGGESTIONS:

1. **Tie literature to history, geography, Biblical principles, and application.**

2. **After reading an unabridged edition, prepare illustrated classics with your older child that can be read to younger children.**

3. **Have a costume party to introduce guests/characters from books.**

4. **Help your child learn to reason cause/effect from literature.**

5. **Avoid books that glorify strife, violence, hatred, etc.**

6. **Don't waste time on books that you have to say *"What's wrong with...?"* (Phil. 4:8)**

The Classics

In this wide reading stage, it's exciting to discover the classics. Why study the classics? There are a number of good reasons. The best I can think of though, is that you can use this material as an instrument for building Christian character and a love of learning in your children.

Remember when I suggested that you establish your reasons for homeschooling? Most of you would say, *"I'm doing this because I want my children to develop Godly character."* So, naturally, what you choose to read or do with your child is based on your philosophy of education. Studying the classics is an excellent way to impart Christian character to your children.

By the way, tie your study of literature to your study of history, geography, Biblical principle and application. Our family tries to read aloud one "great book" with each unit we study.

You may want to have an older child prepare illustrated classics that can be read to younger siblings. The older child will read a longer or unabridged version and create a condensed, picture book classic for the younger child. Certainly, your older child will practice comprehension along the way!

In order to excite interest in reading the classics, you might have a costume party to introduce the guests, whom you invite, to the characters from a particular book. Take on the mannerisms of those characters during the party for fun.

Children absolutely love great literature if they grow up hearing and reading it. They read a classic (or hear you read one aloud) and they want the next and the next — and in the process, they develop a love of learning. Suddenly, videos aren't appealing anymore, because they aren't as descriptive, they don't give enough detail. They are much more shallow. Want your children to fall in love with words? Read the classics.

Help your children reason cause and effect from the literature that you read. As you read aloud to them, help them think about the reasons for things that happen in the book. What choice did the main character make? What were the consequences of his choice?

Avoid books, even classics, that glorify strife, bitterness, and hatred. Remember Philippians 4:8 — We are to choose "whatever is good and pure and holy (and) think on these things." We don't need to waste time on books where we continually have to point out wrong attitudes and behavior (especially where these are portrayed as normal or even admirable.)

Vocabulary

Vocabulary is foundational to learning. Master the vocabulary of a topic and you'll be able to understand what you read about that topic. Learning takes place much more effectively because you have a place to "hang" information.

Master the vocabulary of a discipline, and you will understand that discipline. That's why it is not necessary to study every topic in an area, for example, science. You're learning scientific vocabulary whether you study bees or ants. (Interestingly enough, we can easily test our children's grasp of a unit we have studied by testing vocabulary.)

Vocabulary is best integrated with the units you study — integrated learning is more meaningful to all of us. Words learned in isolation and just regurgitated for a test will be soon forgotten.

Firsthand experiences such as field trips can be used as opportunities to develop meaningful concepts and vocabulary. As you read aloud, ask the child the meaning of words. Use storytelling, oral reading, dramatics, discussions, reports, and conversation to develop vocabulary. Discuss various meanings of familiar words (ex. *strike*.) Overall, teach the meanings of new words in the context of the youngster's studies.

Pupils who need vocabulary development the most can't tell they need it — you must choose vocabulary words for them to study from their reading! When choosing words for your child to study, choose not only difficult words but also simple words. Studying specific definitions for easy words helps your child develop precise thinking.

Dimensions of Vocabulary

Most of us think of writing definitions when we think of vocabulary tests. But there are other aspects of vocabulary to consider. We can vary our style of teaching and testing vocabulary if we know these dimensions.

For example:
- Can the child give synonyms for the word?
  Use a thesaurus or dictionary together to find synonyms.

- Can the child select a particular word to fit into the context? Read a passage aloud to the child leaving out a key word.

- Can your child supply that key word or a synonym for it?

- Finally, can the child understand the root, prefixes, or suffixes of the word? (That is, can he give literal meanings for the parts of the word?) Studying Greek and Latin roots is a great vocabulary booster.

The "slow drip" approach to vocabulary is best. Choose a few words to learn each week and plan to master them. Two to four words can be given on Monday, Tuesday, and Wednesday. (The number of words depends on the age of the child.) Have your child look up and define the words and begin to learn specific meanings of the words. Not only that, let him meet the words repeatedly in his unit studies for the week.

Intentionally use the new words at the dinner table or throughout the day because a word must be met 15 times over a period of three days minimum and be followed with review in order to "stick". Have a test on Friday (oral or written) and encourage the child to use that week's words in his weekly writing.

And of course, remember that the best way to expand vocabulary is through reading.

Plan your approach, relax and have fun watching your children learn. Their vocabulary will mushroom. You see, vocabulary development increases reading ability and wide reading increases vocabulary. (One of the positive self-generating processes in life!)

VOCABULARY DEVELOPMENT

Master the vocabulary of a discipline and you will understand that discipline.

Four Dimensions:
1. **Know a synonym.**
2. **Know a number of meanings for the same word.**
3. **Select a particular meaning that fits into the context.**
4. **Understand word parts: roots, prefixes, suffixes, mostly from Latin and Greek.**

Vocabulary development will increase reading ability and wide reading will increase vocabulary.

REFINEMENT OF READING

This stage of reading begins in junior high (approximately) and continues through adulthood. Critical reading skills develop as students sample various authors, styles of writing, and functions of reading. Study habits mature and vocabularies expand as reading progresses. The refinement stage never ends — we are all in it now.

- **Guidance will be needed in functional reading (ex. reading of specific subject matter) and in reading for deeper meaning.**

- **Literature studies:**
  - **Use a prepared curriculum for an overview.**
  - **Associate literature with historical studies (i.e. when studying history of the world, read the literature of a given period).**
  - **Read stories & fables, biography & autobiography, poetry & narrative, lyric drama.**

- **Study and reference skills:**
  - **book parts**
  - **newspaper parts**
  - **magazines**
  - **dictionary**
  - **thesaurus**
  - **library research**

- **Reading rates:**
  - *skimming rate*: **to review magazine or book, review a familiar story**
  - *rapid reading*: **to re-read the familiar, get the main idea, read quickly for scope of information or look up quick information for temporary use**
  - *normal pace*: **appreciate literary style, read current events**
  - *careful pace*: **to evaluate material, sequence, outline, summarize, paraphrase, memorize, read poetry, judge literary value, master information/details.**

The Refinement Stage of Reading

This stage begins approximately in junior high and continues into adulthood. During adolescence your child becomes a more critical thinker. (Ask any parent of a 12-year-old!) So it follows that he becomes a more critical reader. He samples various author's styles of writing and various reasons for reading. He may learn to read a science textbook in one way, a math book in another way.

This refinement stage never ends: it is constantly maturing. Your child learns purposes for writing and the ways we read for different purposes.

Coping with textbooks
You will probably need to guide your child at first in functional reading in subject areas, especially in textbooks. The child will need to learn how to approach that science or history textbook. The best way he can learn to do this is by the two of you sitting down with those books and walking through them together.

"What are these words in bold print? Am I supposed to think a special way about these words? How do I read this chart, this graph? What about the words under the illustration?" Walk through the process with them so that they learn to read various subject matter.

Literature as literature
All along you've been reading great literature, aloud and silently. Now you may actually add a subject called "literature." A prepared curriculum will include stories, fables, biography, autobiography, poetry, narrative, lyric, and drama. Or if you prefer, continue to read literature as it relates to your thematic studies. Use library book as textbooks.

Reference Skills
Your child will also need to learn reference skills, the parts of a book, newspaper sections, magazines, how to use a dictionary fluently, how to use the thesaurus to improve writing, and library and research skills.

Don't be frightened by library and research skills. If you and your youngster frequent the library together, extending your studies beyond one textbook per subject, you will naturally acquire library references skills. Enlist the help of your librarian to show you how to research topics of interest. It's really painless.

Four rates of reading.
We need to point out to our young readers that we don't read everything at the same speed. We may purposely read rapidly to find short answers to questions or we may need to read purposefully and slowly in technical material.

The *skimming rate* is what we typically use to scan a magazine or book to see if it interests us. We use the *rapid reading rate* to read something with which we are already familiar or to get the main idea. We also use it to read quickly through reams of information to gain an overview on a subject or just to get information which we'll use temporarily. For example, if we are looking up a business in the yellow pages, we read the ads rapidly.

What's the difference between *skimming* and *rapid reading*? When *rapid reading*, our focus is on absorbing content (main ideas, prominent facts, etc..) For *skimming*, just getting a flavor of the text is enough.

The *normal reading rate* is the rate that we use when we want to appreciate a book or an article that we are reading. We don't want to go through it too fast because we really want to enjoy the style and description used by the author. Most people read current events material this way. Or they read normally if they want to be able to retain enough to be able to discuss what was read.

The *careful reading rate* is frequently used by students. Children should probably use this rate when they need to master information or detail, when they need to make judgments about what they read, when they need to be able to re-order or sequence the writing or when they need to retell it in their own words via paraphrase.

The *careful rate* is most often used for reading poetry. Whenever a child has to make a judgment or inference about what he reads, he must read carefully.

Most of us don't notice the differences in reading rate until these are pointed out to us. So, walk through these rates and their purposes with your child. Walk through careful reading of poetry. Help your child learn to pace his reading and both of you will travel easier!

Onward and Upward!
As your student becomes a strong reader — able to ferret out an author's purpose, read critically, paraphrase, summarize, understand various types of literature — he has also picked up a wealth of writing skills as well. But that's our next chapter...

Notes:

In this chapter...

- *Why bother?*

- *Avoiding the agonies..*

- *Mastering the mechanics— grammar, spelling, et al.*

Section Two, Chapter Two

Taking the Worry Out of Writing

If your child can present his ideas in a logical and clear sequence so that people can understand what he means, he will influence our society. He may influence the world.

So you tell me your child freezes when given a writing assignment. Hmm... I wonder. How do you react when asked to write something — say a letter to the editor, or an article for the church newsletter?

If you're like most folks, you freeze up, too!

Now ask yourself, "Why?"

Lack of material? Fear of embarrassment? Uncertainty of how to proceed? Vague feelings of *"I'm not much of a writer"*? Memories of school writing assignments bleeding with red ink?

You may have your own list, but the truth is, most of us learned to see writing as a pain by the end of elementary school. That's sad. And unnecessary. Which makes it doubly sad. In this chapter, we'll explore why this happens so often, how to avoid the pitfalls, and most importantly, how to create writers who communicate their message clearly and powerfully.

Written language is not just mechanics (that is periods in the right place, commas, or apostrophes used correctly) nor is it just grammar, spelling or handwriting workbooks. *Writing is first and foremost a means to communicate!* So let's spend some time thinking about composition and how to encourage children to become writers. Our goal as home educators should be to encourage our children and to lead them into becoming fluent writers.

Writing is one of the most important skills you will ever give your child. If your child can present his ideas in a logical and clear sequence so that people can understand what he means, he will influence our society. He may even influence the world.

I don't think anyone would argue with the fact that writing is becoming a lost art in our society. It's quite easy to use a video to get information, or listen to tapes, *but writing is behind those tapes and videos,* and the simple printed word is one of the most influential elements of communication that we have. (*We're both using it right now, aren't we?*)

Why is it that we do not teach writing? Why don't we produce writers? There are a couple of reasons. First we are too busy. Television, school requirements, worksheets, all rob us of time and writing takes time. It takes time daily in your homeschool. It takes time over a period of months and years to develop fluent writers. And somehow we get lost in the daily busy-ness of life and forget how essential it is to produce writers.

Our forefathers knew the value of writing. Essentially, their education was based on writing. They corresponded regularly, they kept diaries, they copied famous writers, etc., all in order to learn to write better. We can see from our founding fathers' example what a key ingredient writing was in their lives.

What is the most important element of writing? Is it whether the words are spelled correctly? Is it punctuation, handwriting, or sentence structure? The most important element of writing is *thinking time*! And for some reason we don't allow ourselves thinking time in our society.

More often than not, the reason for this is that it seems non-productive to us. We're so keyed in on production, and in our schools sometimes production equals paper work. We're so keyed into this that we have forgotten how valuable thinking time is. We keep our children busy with after school activities and we keep our own calendars full—important meetings, phone calls, things we have to do. The list is endless. And somehow we don't give ourselves time to think. Our busy-ness and our lack of thinking time is robbing us of an essential skill and a valuable tool in our lives.

Writing to Communicate

Why do we write? Why do we teach our children to write? The first purpose is of course, to communicate. There are so many ways to communicate. We communicate when we summarize a science experiment, when we evaluate a book. We communicate when we write a letter to a grandparent or a pen-pal. *The primary purpose of writing is communication.*

Dry as Dust

My daughter wasn't enthusiastic when I asked her to write about any brief topic related to the Egyptian culture. Mummification, chariots, the construction of the pyramids all seemed dull to her.

We all hate busywork and writing for no apparent purpose seemed like busywork to Ashley. Though I reminded her that it would seem even more like busywork to write out answers for those end-of-chapter questions in a typical high school history book, I understood her point of view.

How about a more relevant purpose for writing for a fifteen year old girl? After some discussion, she decided upon a writing topic: EGYPTIAN COSMETICS AND BEAUTIFICATION. Ashley read between the lines in dozens of library reference books about Egypt for enough information for a paper. How appropriate! What eye-openers for us in the 20th century who think we are the inventors of red fingernail polish! *Did she have an interested audience? You bet!* The entire family was fascinated by her descriptions of Egyptian beautification techniques.

Dry as Dust II

Eight year old Heather was preparing her insect display for family night recently. She wrote the following note to attach to the box: *"Do not tuch."* I got the message but seized the opportunity for expansion. *Heather wanted to communicate.* Was there some way to build on that?

"Heather," I said, "why have you written that note?"

"Because, Mom, you know those insects will break if someone touches them."

"Why is that, Heather?"

"Because all of the juice has dried out of them, I guess."

"Oh, let me see if I heard what you said. 'Do not touch these insects. They are dry and fragile.' What if I write those words on this card and you copy them to attach to your insect collection?"

Moral of these two dry stories? **Writing is for communication. Writers need a message to communicate and an audience to write for.**

There is also a by-product especially valuable to home educators. *We learn by writing!* When we write, we organize our thoughts, we think and we actually learn. When we have a child explain in writing the procedure used for a math equation or how to make a craft, he's thinking while he is writing. As he thinks, the ideas jell in his mind and become a part of him.

When a child takes notes about the sermon on Sunday morning, or notes from a book, or notes from a video that tells how to do something, that child is thinking. Taking notes requires thinking.

[In fact, it's a good idea to make notes in the margin as you read this manual. As you write, you will be more inclined to think through (and remember) ways to apply these concepts to your specific situation.]

The benefits of writing for learning make it a very powerful tool in every teacher's kit. *On the other hand, be careful to handle it wisely as this tool cuts both ways. Remember, unless your youngster sees this writing assignment as a real-life way of communicating, it will be another case of "dreaded writing drudgery," ... a deathblow to fluent, effective writing.*

What Should We Write About?

Writing is for real life. Writing *"a story about the line drawing of the purple elephant in your workbook"* is not real life and children detect that immediately. On the other hand, if their written ideas are affecting others, they become more eager to write.

What are real life examples of writing? The list is endless. Notes, letters, journals, and prayers are good for starters.

Write notes to your youngsters that require an answer. For example, *"David, will you join me on Saturday morning for an ice-cream cone date? What flavor will you order? Love, Dad."* David, who is seven-years-old, writes an acceptance to Dad. It has to be longer than just yes or no because Dad asked another question.

Letters can include descriptive paragraphs of just about anything your child experiences. Our family visited the zoo this summer. The gorillas were especially entertaining that day. One even tried to kiss Meg (4) through the glass window. Meg dictated a paragraph to me describing the gorilla's kiss and included the paragraph in a letter to grandmother. What grandmother wouldn't enjoy hearing about the giant gorilla with black lips that tried to kiss her granddaughter?

Letters might also include an explanation of how a science project was done or a narrative about losing one's tooth. Grandparents, pen-pals, or shut-ins are good recipients for these letters.

Persuasive letters about moral topics can be written to policymakers or editors. Our children's writing can begin affecting others now!

Journal writing can be free-lance. For starters, the child can begin to write prayers. Habitual morning quiet times are conducive to writing directly to God who listens. Or, your child may be inspired to write about the freshly fallen snow after listening to you read poems on the same subject. Set the timer for 15 or 20 minutes and let the child write anything. Unless it is too personal, he will probably want to share it. Be an audience!

Only after much practice in freeflow writing, should we introduce more academic writing projects such as poetry, news reports, book reviews, short stories, or research. Ease into these projects with your child. If you're like me, you'll be learning how to write along with your child. The good news is that the books will teach you, too!

The very young child, such as the kindergartner who's just learning to write may begin by copying words, phrases or sentences that you write. The next step would be writing from dictation. This approach will benefit even children who are writing on their own.

WHAT DO WE WRITE?

Stumped for writing ideas?   Try this list for starters.
Remember to always use the writing in some way.

- directions to one's home

- news reports

- book reviews

- prayers

- copying passages of scripture

- speeches or oral presentations

- friendly letters

- letters to the editor or policymakers

- letters to a sick friend

- letters for freebies

- notes

- greeting cards

- invitations

- thank you notes

- journals

- dictated words, sentences, paragraphs

- copying short passages of great literature

- lists of adjectives to describe something studied

- shopping lists, toy lists, etc.

- explanations: (*How to run the washing machine.*
  Write and post in the laundry room.)

- descriptions (*Describe the snakeskin you touched.*)

- relating events (*Tell about the squirrel that got in our pantry.*)

- persuasion (*Why do you think you should be allowed to*
  watch family videos on Friday nights?)

"What am I going to dictate?" you ask? Educator Ruth Beechick suggests dictating short passages of literature. Passages can be as short as a sentence or as long as a paragraph. After the child writes from dictation, he compares what he has written to what was written by the author to see any punctuation or spelling differences.

To take this a step further, the child can read a passage, put the passage away, and try to rewrite it in his own words. He can compare his writing to the original author's writing to see the differences in the author's words, descriptions, punctuation or sentence order. (This is the way some of our forefathers such as Benjamin Franklin learned to write — and how many professional writers continue to learn.)

GOALS FOR WRITING

Correct Expression
punctuation
grammar
capitalization
spelling

Clear, Logical Organization
introduction
expansion
conclusion

Precise, Meaningful Words
Complete Sentences, Paragraphs

Maturity
dialogue
moral theme
humor
character development

Developing and Coaching Young Writers

Many homeschool parents dread teaching writing more than they dread writing itself. Why? Because down deep inside, we hate to see our kids go through what we did — the cramped hand from that cursive handwriting book, the drudgery of writing a 2,500-word essay on some topic we didn't know anything about (or care to), the despair of seeing it again swimming in red ink, the agony of correcting and re-writing it, perhaps even worse, the embarrassment of having a piece we really did care about picked apart or dismissed off-hand!

No wonder we turn white when someone asks us to write that article for the church newsletter!

Relax! We don't have to do that to our youngsters, if we will be aware of potential stumbling blocks along the way and take a little time to think through our task:

- *What are we aiming for?*
- *How does a writer develop?*
- *How can we help our young writer(s) master the basic mechanics — spelling, grammar, handwriting, etc. ?*

What are we aiming for?

You can't expect to teach everything there is to know about writing to any child in one year. This is something that takes time to develop. (Professional writers assure us the process never ends.)

So what are we aiming for as we teach composition? Certainly the point is not to finish a grammar workbook! Those who teach and research language tell us not to expect correctness of expression — correct punctuation, grammar, capitalization, spelling — until the later stages of maturity. They tell us that we should strive first of all for our children to organize their thoughts so that they can be presented clearly and logically.

There is more than one way to teach your child to organize thoughts logically and clearly. I jokingly tell people that if you have a child with an organized closet, you'll have a child who can think logically and present his ideas logically on paper.

Do you remember the suggestion to emphasize language experience for preschoolers and beginning readers? Such exercises not only prepare the child to read, but also teach them to compose, organize and sequence a story in a way that is understandable by the reader. So use oral language experience to undergird writing and reading.

Experts tell us that mature writing often includes titles, paragraphs, or dialogue. Perhaps the best possible model for the very

SAMPLE WRITING CHECKLIST

This list includes only what one Mom thought was most important for a particular child in a particular year. It was done for a sixth grader and kept in that child's 3-ring binder for the entire year as a reminder when writing. Be sure to make your own personalized list.

Use capital letters for important words and for the first and last words in the title.

Write the title on the first line, then skip a line before you begin to write your story.

Have an interesting beginning sentence.

Have a sentence to close your paper.

Use sentences between thoughts to make a connection (transition sentences).

Use interesting words. Use the thesaurus to help you ("dollar" verbs and colorful adjectives).

Tell everything that happened in order.

Begin each sentence with a capital letter.

Do you need capitals anywhere else?

Use commas, semi-colons, periods, question marks, apostrophes, hyphens, and quotation marks correctly.

Leave margins at the top and bottom and on the edges of your paper. Start your writing on the correct side of the paper.

Write neatly using italic handwriting.

Check your spelling. As you write, if you are unsure of a word, put a light dot on it and come back during the revision stage to correct it.

young child for these skills would be for you to compose a story together, especially if that story is based on a field trip or an event just experienced. The child re-tells in sequence the event. Together you decide on a title. You are modeling how to write the title with capitals for important words and how the title should reflect what will be in the story. You write as the child dictates and he sees how words make sentences and sentences make paragraphs and paragraphs change as you change ideas. You are also modelling how a story should have a definite beginning and ending as you write together.

How do I know *you know* how to do all this? Because you are an adult and you think like an adult. You won't be satisfied with a story without some sort of introduction, even if it is one sentence, and some sort of wrap up.

As the child's writing matures, you may see him including a moral theme in his stories. He may begin to include moral themes after reading good literature that depicts godly character traits or after discussing noble ideas which come up in the classics you are reading aloud. Reading great literature will carry over into your child's writing.

Use school breaks (such as summer vacation) to read teacher helps that will teach you to teach writing skills. (See appendix). Then take the time to prayerfully list a few writing goals for each of your children. You might be at the stage where you want your children to remember periods and capitals. Or you might have older children who need to include more details in their writing or use more descriptive, less-overused words. You may have a child who is having a really tough time with spelling. The priority this year seems to be working on words frequently misspelled. Take time to stop, listen to the Holy Spirit, ask him to illumine your mind, and reveal to you the priorities for your child in writing this year.

Writing is a process but you will see milestones as your child develops. *Readiness for writing begins at birth.* The child listens as you speak and he learns grammar. He learns how English sentences are constructed. One thing leads to another and by the time the child's around five, he's able to dictate stories to you. Those stories, whether he recognizes it or not, are made of sentences.

During this readiness period, read aloud to the child so that he can hear word and sentence patterns.

The next milestone is beginning writing. At what age should a child begin composition? Even toddlers are beginning writers. When a toddler can hold a pencil and scribble a letter, he can often tell you exactly what he wrote. That is beginning composition. When you write the text as a child narrates an event (visit to the bakery, visit to a park, etc.), that is beginning composition. A child is never too young to compose.

A beginning writer is just interested in expressing himself. He is not really interested in producing a formal product. Of course he will have bizarre spelling for a while — my suggestion to you is to *simply enjoy it.* Enjoy those love notes with the crazy spelling.
So cute! This won't last forever and when you both look back in ten years you'll have such fun.

Not only may his spelling be bizarre, but he may be completely unaware of capitalization and punctuation errors. Not even seeing his mistakes. *That's just as it should be!* This is not the time to point them out. Use the opportunity to encourage your child to write, write, write.

You may have a son (or daughter) who has trouble with small motor coordination. Producing letters with a pencil is too painful. Support him by allowing him to dictate more stories. You have him copy one sentence and you copy the rest for him. Or have him dictate stories into a tapeplayer. Again, you write most of it and have him write a sentence or two. Or use magnetic letters or letter cards to have him "write" words from your dictation. Don't skip writing experience altogether because it is hard. Be creative in getting this experience into him. (Later you can teach reluctant handwriters to type.)

At some point, your writer will begin to notice his mistakes in spelling, grammar, etc. *It is very easy for the child to become discouraged now because he realizes that good composition is not just writing ideas but also mechanics.* Don't let this drag him down. Help him with just one or two types of errors at a time.

Start with *periods* and *capitals*. Are the periods in place? Are the letters capitalized at the beginning of the sentence? As these are mastered, help him with other types of errors.

Keep mental or anecdotal notes of the words that the child misspells and include those words at a different time on a spelling list rather than going through everything he has written and marking with red pencil all the words he has misspelled. Keep your own running ledger of the words he has misspelled and later give those words for practice. Are hand held spelling calculators okay? Yes, for a quick spell check. Spelling calculator games might even motivate your child to practice spelling drills.

[By the way, your phonics study together with a beginning reader is also that child's spelling program. (As mentioned in the last chapter, this is another good reason to teach phonics.) Dictate short phonetic word lists.]

Ever wonder why all of a sudden a child begins to recognize mechanical and spelling errors? Typically, your child will read fluently before he can recognize spelling errors in his own writing. That is simply because his visual memory has not caught up with his decoding skills.

As he moves into the wide reading stage, he begins to see the differences in his writing and the writing he sees in books which he reads. He makes comparisons. He notices that he doesn't spell words correctly, or that his punctuation is terrible. This is when many of us first say *"Writing...Yuk!"* (Few of us enjoy failing.) Mark papers occasionally, but be gentle and supportive of the young writer's efforts.

Don't discourage your child by over-emphasizing mechanics! Continue to encourage him and require him to write something each day — even if it's just a few sentences dictated or 15 minutes of free-lance journal writing.

Gradually the child becomes an independent writer. He knows how to evaluate and correct his own papers, and where to go for help on writing mechanics (grammar handbook, dictionary, etc.)

For example, if he is not sure of a verb tense, he knows where that grammar manual is and how to use it to find the correct verb form. Or he knows how to use the dictionary to find puzzling words. At this point a person can edit his own work. From here on, only motivation and refinement determine just how effective a communicator he becomes.

"Parts is Parts, Right?"

When educators look at how a certain type of learning develops, they often try to break it down into components as well. What makes up writing? Written language includes thoughts, spelling and vocabulary, along with handwriting and grammar. The most important component is THOUGHT. But always remember that written language is integrated.

We can't just teach the parts and expect to produce writers. Somehow, in our society, we've adopted a factory approach to learning. We've adopted the notion that if we give our children grammar workbooks, if they learn all the parts of speech and all the noun functions, if we give them spelling workbooks and lists of spelling words for tests on Friday, if we give them workbooks with ideas for creative writing — somehow we think that if we mix all the right parts together — that in the end we'll come out with a polished creative writer. (Okay, you're right... we'd probably settle for someone who could write a letter.)

This is a carryover, I believe, from the days when Henry Ford made such great strides in producing automobiles through the factory approach. But children are human beings. Human beings are not like automobiles. You don't assemble parts and expect a product. Writing is integrated. All of its parts are linked and the one sure way to produce good writers is by having them write— simply WRITE.

Easing into Writing

How can we ease into writing with our children so that the whole process won't seem like such a chore? Young children and reluctant writers must be encouraged lest they stumble along the way.

Before even picking up the pencil, take ample time to discuss the project. Pull information from your child by questioning. As you pull the information, jot ideas, words, or phrases on a chalkboard or paper using the child's own words, you're developing a framework for the child's writing. We call this pre-writing.

> *"Amy, describe our dissection of the owl pellets."*

> "Mom, you know I thought that pellet looked like a blob of nothing at first. All I saw was matted hair on the outside."

> (I'm busy writing her phrases on the board as she speaks.)
> *"What did you think?"*

> "I thought it was going to be boring."

> *"Were you disappointed?"*

> "No, it took only a few seconds to start finding bones. Then we couldn't find enough. Carrie and I found enough bones to put together a whole vole skeleton and Jay found a mouse's jaw."

> *"What did the jaw look like? "How did you identify the mouse jaw? "Were there any smells? "What did it feel like to touch the pellet?"*

You get the picture. By dialoguing during this prewriting stage you pull information from the child. Sketch the ideas on paper and let the child later use the sketch as an outline. Does the child's description make sense to you? Ask questions for details.

After the initial writing, you and the child can go back to use vivid, concise words. *"What is another word for put together?" "How about* **reconstruct***? Let's look together in the thesaurus."*

When your child writes and you read it, ask lots of questions about what he wrote to show that you are genuinely interested. If you do this, he will be more inclined to add specific words or include more describing words that you want him to use.

All writing, even fiction, should relate to our experiences. It is much easier to paint a vivid word picture of something we have actually seen or experienced. We experience what we can sense—our sights, feelings, what we hear or smell or touch. Children have experiences every day and none is too trivial to write about. *"Listen. Describe the rain as it hits the roof." "Tell an ill friend of*

ENCOURAGING AND TRAINING YOUNG WRITERS

Writers become writers by writing —
every day but not always in the same format.

Encourage free-lance writing. Allow ample time for thinking.

Have the young child tell you stories which you write.

Write about what you have experienced, even in creative writing of stories.

Allow the product to cool before revision.
Final work should be neat, legible, have even spacing and proper alignment.

Limit workbooks.

Limit quick answers.

Ask why and how questions about your child's writing which will encourage observation skills so they will add description and detail.

Make booklets, scrapbooks.

Model writing for your child.

Bear the load with a child who has poor fine motor skills —
take turns writing.

Play lots of word games.

Use a "spider web" for pre-writing.

your feelings of sadness for her." "What does it feel like to touch baby brother's soft skin?" Our job is to draw out these experiences and help our children put them on paper.

How can we motivate a child who seems to have *no* interest in writing? Change your approach. Tell him why we write. Make sure his writing is affecting someone, that there will be an audience for what he writes. Make sure that he is writing about something that interests him. If writing an entire paper or even a paragraph seems overwhelming, construct sentences together at first.

Take simple sentences you have written and expand them together for practice. For example, "The man drove the car." *What kind of man? A fireman, the father, a busdriver?* "The *deliveryman* drove the car." *What is a word that will express more clearly how he drove?* "The deliveryman *toured the city* in his car." *What kind of car. Tell me something that will give me a clear picture of the car.* (Writing is painting word pictures.) "The delivery-man toured the city in *his boss's limousine.""Aha, now I see."* Discussion exercises like this may loosen up a reluctant writer.

Carry the load with him.
From that point, build combined sentences into paragraphs with a single main idea, and later longer papers. Wherever there is difficulty, bear the burden with the child. The learning curve always goes up if an activity is slightly easy rather than slightly difficult.

A child's awareness of mechanics (grammar, punctuation, spelling), lags slightly behind his ability to read. In other words, he will reach the point where he can read much more that he can actually write. *Content and process* are much more important than *product* at this point. Ignore ridiculous spelling for awhile. **Papers bleeding with red ink are an inspiration to no one.**

Distinguish Formal vs. Informal
Even as your young writer matures, it's still best to let him focus as much as possible on content. That's why it's important for you as teacher to distinguish between the two basic types of written language — formal and informal. When giving assignments, decide first whether the project will be formal or informal.

The goal of informal writing is to produce a flow of ideas. It emphasizes *process* rather than *product*. When you have your child summarize information you have just read to him about an artist you're studying, that is informal writing.

WHAT'S A MOTHER TO DO?

Case Study I

James, grade five, keeps his creative writing to a minimum. His goal is to finish the assignment— he is not particularly concerned with writing interesting papers. What should his mother do? First of all, examine your approach to the assignment. Reluctant writers may need lots of support. Choose a mutually agreed upon topic about which to write. Who will read or listen to the writing? Agree upon an audience: the family, grandparents who will receive a letter, a children's newsletter, etc. Discuss what James knows about the topic. Sketch his ideas on a chalkboard as you talk, clustering ideas that seem to go together (paragraphs to be). Act excited about the project even if James seems unhappy. For a while, you may have to go even further by actually composing sentences with James using the "outline" you have made together. Actually write the paper with James. Allow the paper to cool for a day. The next day, revise sentences together for a better flow and use a thesaurus together to find vivid words. This is bearing the burden with an unwilling writer.

Case Study II

Karen has a daughter who wants to write a piece once, never to be revised again. *What should she do? First, I wouldn't make that daughter revise every piece that is written but I* would *have her write something each day. Then, on days when a revision is in order, I'd make a point to tell the child that she is not writing a new piece today because a revision is in order and that in order to allow enough time for revision I'm deleting several other things she would be doing that day.* What a privilege! *(i.e.* What a motivator!*) Mom is allowing time for the creative process to work!*

- *Effective communication is the goal.*
- *Content and process are more important than mechanics.*

Informal writing should be done frequently. The child writes about what he has read or about an activity just finished. It can be letter writing or writing an outline for an oral report that must be given.

Usually informal writing does not need to be re-written. Corrections can usually be made on the original, though on rare occasions it may be appropriate for your child to re-write a paper with obvious mistakes. Examples of informal writing that you *would not* correct are diary or journal entries or love notes to Dad.

Formal writing is product oriented. It's written for presentation to an audience. Therefore, more emphasis is placed on proper grammar and punctuation. Formal writing should be neat and legible with proper spacing and alignment. *Formal writing requires editing and revision and is always rewritten.* You can see that formal writing comes later in the elementary years.

An example of formal writing would be a research paper. Occasionally, you may consider a book review formal writing.

Formal writing has steps. First is the *thinking* stage. Brainstorm with your child to help him collect ideas and organize his thoughts. Second, is the stage when the child writes just for content—just to get those *ideas on paper*.

Third comes *revision*. (This works best when it is not done the same day. Allow a cooling period of a day or so before starting revision.) The child goes back, looks at the flow, looks at the mechanics, and makes the necessary changes. This is often where you step in and help him to see how to revise. The final steps in formal writing are *re-writing* and often a *publishing/presentation* stage where the written text is packaged visually or orally for the final audience.

Formal writing takes lots of time and effort. (*Believe me!—I know.*) Anyone would be frustrated if he thought every piece of writing had to be formal. Use both informal and formal writing.

STEPS FOR FORMAL WRITING

THINK (experience, research, brainstorm)

WRITE (content most important)

REVISE (flow and mechanics)

REWRITE (next day)

PUBLISH/PRESENT (writing is for an audience)

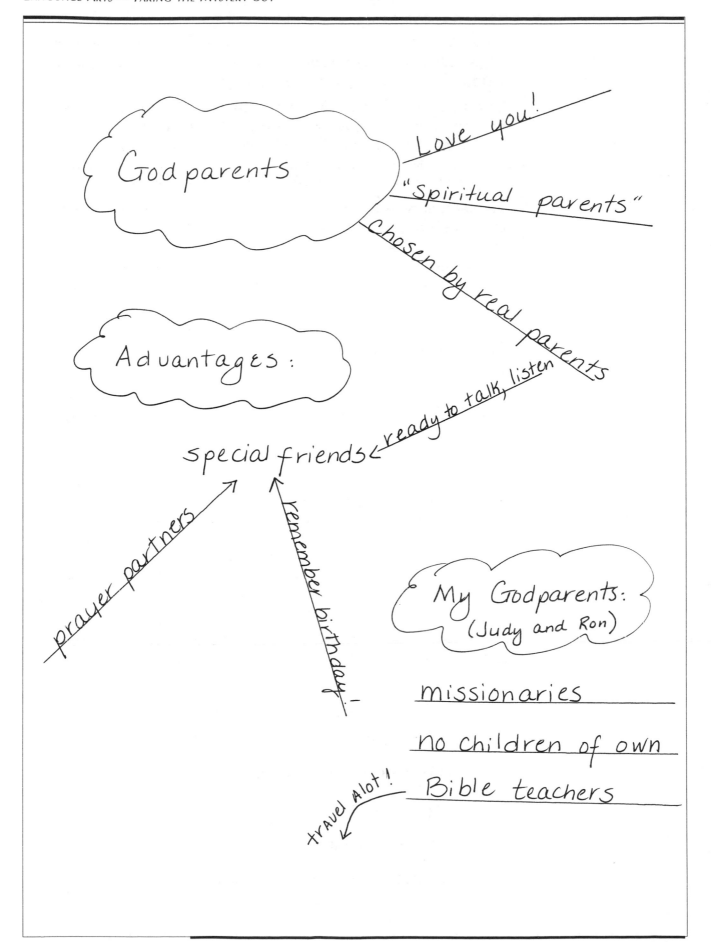

Capturing Ideas

A "spider web" is a useful pre-writing tool. You take ideas and instead of doing the formal (I, II, III, a, b, c) approach to outlining, you outline your ideas with simple phrases and extend these ideas so that they are all on one page (see opposite page.) The outline resembles a spider web because lines are going in all directions. You are diagramming what you will be writing about. (Much more visual.) Use color to highlight important parts or headings and be creative. It's a lot more fun that the old-fashioned traditional outline.

Share the experience

My friends and I have recently discovered the benefits of having a children's weekly writing club. One mother leads the group which gathers to share writing. After teaching briefly about an idea, such as using vivid language, spider webbing, or using a thesaurus, we assign a starter topic. (For example, *write a description of your bedroom* or *tell an unusual popcorn experience.)*

The children then take time to write a rough draft on paper and share it with the group. Listeners are encouraged to ask questions and the young writers are inspired to clarify and explain better. We have found the writing club an inspiration to our children which we alone could not provide. Remember: writing is for an audience. *When your child sees that his writing affects someone, he will be more likely to write.*

Our children need to see us writing. Some home schooling families have decided to have an evening that they call letter writing night. Everyone sits at the kitchen for a night of writing letters to senators, relatives or prison inmates. Just as we must model reading, we must model writing to our children in order for them to become natural writers.

Mastering the Mechanics

The mechanics of writing — spelling, grammar, punctuation, even handwriting — are simply tools for us as readers and writers, standardizing our language for more effective communication. (For example, it's easier to give and receive written information when there are standard spellings for words.) To use another metaphor, such details do not fuel the engine of written communication, but lubricate it.

Once your youngster has learned the satisfaction of writing to communicate with an audience he wants to reach, he'll want his message to shine through.

It's not difficult to find textbooks, manuals, worksheets, etc. that focus on mechanics. But realistically, the best way to teach mechanics is to help your child perfect work that he's already written.

Of course, we need to do this in a non-threatening way. Not *"I'm over you and I'm marking this with red pencil so you better get it right this time because I'm tired of these mistakes."* It's *"I'm here to help you do this. I'm on your team. Now let's work on this together and talk about this together and produce a great paper!"* You walk your child through the re-write. You coach and encourage. He's not going to get out of an assignment (after all, you're the authority and you know what's best for his school day) but you can help bear the burden.

Some families choose to have the child write something new each day, but at the end of the week, ask the child to turn in only one of his items for polishing. Over the weekend you would edit the work for errors. On Monday morning, you might sit down with the child and discuss how it could be better rewritten. Pull sentences from the paper, write them with the errors on the blackboard and together correct mistakes. For some children it takes the pressure away if you use the blackboard instead of the child's paper. Discuss only what's on the child's level when doing this rewriting.

For example, for very young children emphasize punctuation, capitalization, and a few spelling words. For an older child, discuss how to develop paragraphs, how to make the sentences flow more smoothly, or how to combine sentences so that they are not so choppy. After this polishing and revision, the child copies the work in his best handwriting and it is saved. At the end of a semester, "publish" the work that you have refined. Can you see all that you have accomplished in this exercise? You have done spelling, punctuation, composition, and even handwriting as you have the child recopy in his best handwriting. Why not have him copy it in italic when his handwriting matures to that point?

Did you notice that I said nothing about using a workbook to teach mechanics? Keep workbook instruction in its place. For short 'seasons', you will be spending a few months on intensive word usage and punctuation and capitalization.

Spelling

Your child's initial spelling exercises come from his phonics instruction lists. He is learning to write from dictation the same words he is learning to read.

Dictate simple words or sentences. The child will write these on the blackboard or paper. At some point, your child's reading ability will exceed his spelling ability. He will be able to read words which he cannot spell. What's next?

At first allow a little creativity in spelling. Then, as you continue to work through phonics lists, he'll begin to notice when words look funny. That's the time to try an efficient, effective approach to teaching spelling. Your child will probably be about grade three and you have finished working through dictated phonics lists. His spelling is no longer totally bizarre. He does not misspell every other word. This is the best time to develop spelling lists from the child's own mistakes.

There are two ways to individualize spelling lists. In the first, the child keeps a running list in the back of his 3-ring binder of words which he frequently misspells in his writing. Because he notices when words don't look right, he can easily turn to that list for quick reference of confusing words.

The second way to teach individualized spelling uses a composition notebook. In that notebook, you write each spelling rule, one rule per page. (Not up to producing your own spelling rule book? See Resource List for one entitled "Tricks of the Trade.") Each time the child misspells a word, that word is placed under the appropriate rule. This forces the child to analyze words more closely and enables both you and the child to see problem areas clearly. You may use this for words misspelled on pre-tests given at the beginning of a workbook lesson or for words misspelled in the child's writing.

There is nothing wrong with allowing your child to ask you how to spell a word of which he is unsure. There's no reason to force him to look up every word he doesn't know in a dictionary. (Stop and think about what *you* do if you don't know how to spell a word. The first thing you do is go to someone you think might know the spelling. You, too, think that is easier than using the dictionary.)

Teach your child to think while spelling and spell by syllables, not by rote like parrots. If he spells by syllables and writes each syllable as he says it (either aloud or in his mind), he is more likely to spell the word correctly.

Teach your child to clearly pronounce each syllable of a word. If you have a child who is mispronouncing a word frequently, he will probably spell it as he pronounces it rather than correctly. Analyze with your child reasons for misspelling a word.

For example, if you do use a spelling workbook and start your week on Monday with a pre-test on that week's words, look closely together at misspelled words. Talk about how the word was misspelled, whether it was an error in pronunciation of the word, whether it was an error in reversing some letters in the word, or not being aware of the phonics rule.

Look for clues. If you have to, make up something silly. For example, the word 'piece' has pie in it so you can always remember piece is spelled *p-i-e*-c-e.

Do you know one technique good spellers use to remember letters that have a schwa sound? For example 'abundant.' Is it spelled with an *e* or an *a*? (No fair looking back!) A naturally good speller will look at that word and purposely say it wrong when spelling it. He has a visual memory of the word and he says it in his mind, abund*A*nt, instead of abund*E*nt. You may need to point this technique out to your child if he's not already doing it on his own.

To teach those who have a real problem with spelling, you'll need to insure that spelling words enter the child's long term memory with lots of practice.

Have the child look at and analyze the word with you as I've already explained. Also explain how to say the word *aloud* the way it looks in order to remember irregular spellings. Then have him practice the word. (First, by writing it 5 times while looking at the word, saying each letter as it is written. Then by writing it 5 times without looking at it, again saying each letter as it is written. And finally, by writing the word with eyes closed, again saying each letter as it is written.) Use the blackboard, rather than pencil and paper for this exercise. The large muscles get used, which seems to help kinesthetic learners, and it's easier on the hands.

Words should be practiced daily for one week, then tested, and a review test given every four weeks. It takes that much practice and maybe even more for the word to enter the long term memory.

Have frequent, even daily, spelling drills with budding spellers. Teach phonetically regular words first and follow with frequently used sight words. Your lists can come from the phonics material you used to teach reading or you can use lists in resource books.

In addition to individualized spelling lists and daily word drills have the child spell words related to his unit studies. These would be his spelling challenge lists. For example, if you are studying the human body, words like *skeleton*, *digestion*, and *diaphragm* could be both spelling and vocabulary words for the week.

Handwriting

Handwriting instruction begins with printing and leads to cursive. You have several paths from which to choose. The traditional route begins with *ball and stick* print and leads to *traditional cursive handwriting* such as Palmer. Or, you may choose *precursive* which leads to *simplified cursive* such as D'Nealian handwriting. Finally, you may choose *italic print* which leads to *connected italic* handwriting. What are the differences?

Printing has three basic forms. One is the *ball and stick* or a modification thereof. Here the young child is taught to form letters using big circles and lines. (Very young children find it easy to draw only lines or circles.) Another form, *precursive hand-writing* has style and legibility. Precursive handwriting tries to use, as far as possible one motion for each letter rather than picking the pencil up and putting it back down again. The idea is that this will help some children overcome reversals, especially of the letters 'b' and 'd'. (If your child really has a perceptual problem this is not always going to work. I've seen such children still make the 'b' or 'd' in reverse in one motion.)

Italic printing can be started in the early grades and developed in later grades into *connected italic cursive*. Italic handwriting uses only ellipses and lines to produce letters. It is distinctively attractive and legible, and some feel the ellipse is easier to make than a perfect circle for young children. (One of the keys to success when using italic handwriting is not to introduce the ink pen too early. Use pencil for a long time until the strokes are mastered.)

You can begin italic instruction in kindergarten. Children love it. While you're at it you can learn along with the children.

Traditional cursive (such as the Palmer Method) is typically American. It was taught to you, most likely, when you were in school. *Simplified cursive* is taught in some handwriting texts.

Printing >>>>>>>>>>>> Cursive
Ball/stick >>>>>>>>>>>>>> *traditional* *precursive* >>>>>>>>>>>>> *simplified cursive*
italic print >>>>>>>>>>>>> *connected italic*

Teach the child who has extreme difficulty with small motor skills to type. As soon as he can read well, he is ready for typing instruction. Allow your child to type reports and papers. Along the way, also teach your child to use a word processor. He'll appreciate these skills when he has longer reports.

Grammar

I close this section with a discussion of grammar. Why so late in the discussion? Because there is a tendency for too many of us to think that grammar equals writing instruction. By now you know better. Think — *composition equals writing*.

As already discussed, *spelling, handwriting,* and *grammar* are merely supplemental — helping our writing be more effective in connecting with our readers.

Grammar includes punctuation, capitalization, usage, parts of speech, and noun functions. The best place to learn grammar is in the context of revising an essay. Teach grammar through the child's writing.

Every child comes to school already knowing plenty of grammar. More often than not, he uses the correct subject with the correct verb form. He uses the parts of speech accurately. Our job is just to iron out the wrinkles.

Use one complete and compact resource for a season of grammar instruction. There is no reason to re-teach grammar day after day and year after year. Teaching, reteaching, and overpracticing it is redundant (and counter-productive!) One year, not eight, is all it will take. Let's keep grammar in its place and not confuse it with writing.

It's all one package...

So what's included in a homeschooler's language arts program? First, there's reading. If the child is young, you are teaching phonics. If he's older, he's reading good literature and non-fiction on his own. In addition, you're reading aloud daily to your children, young and old. Read good literature and books related to the units you are studying. Each day you're studying vocabulary — not long lists of words, just a few. Memory work is important, so he will memorize definitions in addition to scripture or occasional poetry.

Your child will also be writing something daily. Young children will dictate stories or experiences for you to write. Beginning readers will write words or short sentences from dictation. Paragraphs or reports will be written by the older child. Writing will relate to his experiences and subject matter. It will communicate.

For short periods of time, say a few weeks, you will teach grammar units. This will take time from your writing so you won't want to do it every day except for perhaps a quick drill. (No more than 10 minutes.) You will teach spelling daily. Teach phonetically regular lists first, learning the rules of spelling as you go. Also include words personally misspelled in the child's personal compositions. Finally, add words that relate to the unit of study. Merge the lists with the subject being studied for meaningfulness.

Do you see how you can streamline your planning for language arts if you think in these terms? Think of what your child needs and be ready to revise written plans on a day to day basis if necessary.

Think of accomplishing goals rather than working through mounds of workbooks and curriculum guides. In a while, the above exercises will become daily habits. You will know what you are doing in reading and written language each day. This takes less time and still accomplishes your purpose!

DAILY READING HABITS

Phonics as Needed

Good Literature — aloud and silent

Books Related to Unit Study

Vocabulary Memory Work

DAILY WRITING HABITS

YOUNGER - dictate stories, write words, sentences from dictation

OLDER - write each day!

Quick Spelling Review (5 minutes)

Grammar and Handwriting for a season!

Notes:

Notes:

In this section...

- **Real-life learning**

- **Exploring together**

- **Math made easy**

Section Three
Pulling It All Together

Our task is to cultivate problem-solvers who know how to retrieve and use information.

As we head into the next century, we find ourselves in the midst of a massive information explosion. Today, computers make more information available than we could ever absorb. There's no lack of information and we'll never learn it all. In fact, why should we? Information we learn today may be outdated tomorrow. Besides, we can always find out what we don't know. Yet, our adult literacy rate is at an all-time low. And common sense has become a rare commodity.

With our founding fathers, it was far different. In those days of widespread literacy, the person with the most facts had the upper hand. Every new bit of information they learned was jealously hoarded — a species of apple — weather data — a new star sighted. Thomas Jefferson carried a notebook in his pocket. In that notebook, he recorded every new fact he learned. Since he was interested in everything from astronomy to architecture, and recorded much information, he was considered one of the most learned men of his day.

The person with the most facts stored in his brain is no longer considered the most intelligent. Something more is needed to be well-educated. Besides, there is no human being who can absorb all the data now available. Computers can retrieve information and manipulate columns of numbers much more efficiently than any white-collar worker. The challenge today is applying facts and solving problems.

Learning is more than collecting knowledge and memorizing math tables. Our task as parents and teachers is to cultivate problem-solvers with common sense who can retrieve and use pertinent information as it's needed. We must teach our child-ren to create, to explore, to discern. So let's look at the exciting challenge of learning and exploring together as a family.

In this chapter...

- ## Real-life learning

- ## Just what are "Unit Studies" anyway?

- ## Seeing the big picture

LEARNING AND EXPLORING TOGETHER

Section Three, Chapter One

Learning and Exploring Together

Young people who learn to think, to discern, to communicate will be the adults who will impact our society. Who knows? This generation may be God's special servants in training.

In days past, the person with the most facts was the smartest. Today, self-reliant problem-solvers are at a premium. Why?

During the Industrial Revolution, we learned that an assembly line was useful for producing top-notch machinery in an efficient manner. Similarly, we began to think that if an assembly line approach was good for machinery, it would be good for producing educated humans, too! We began to reason that if we could just put in the right facts and information at the right grade level — *Behold!* — at the end of 12 years we'd have an "educated" citizen.

In an attempt to keep up with all the factual information available, our textbooks began to "cover" mounds of information. A single history book would cover the explorers, the colonists, the Revolutionary War, and on to the modern period, all in one year even on the elementary level. We call those *survey courses*.

They look good because those scope and sequence charts have so much listed on them. It looks like the children are learning a lot. (In this way our textbooks reflect our present fast-paced society, if nothing else.) But what really happens? The information is rapidly covered—just touched upon. In an attempt to learn everything we learn nothing in depth.

Even if we could memorize all the facts available to us in the information explosion, would that create in us a *curiosity explosion*? Evidently not. High school teachers complain that their students are just saying, *"Tell me what I need to know to pass the test. That's all I want. Don't ask me to do more."*

An assembly line approach to education doesn't work for a number of reasons. We are living in the information age. No one can (or wants to) absorb all the data available to us. And factory teaching produces followers, not thinkers. Finding and memorizing facts is taught, but not thinking. *"Just give me the grade so I can get out of here."*

Today, business executives tell us they don't need graduates filled with facts. Instead, they ask for graduates with skill to retrieve and organize information so it can be used. What does our society need? Individuals who can creatively develop new ways of doing things — people who can take information which is readily available, and do something with it from start to finish. As one educator put it, *"If we don't help people learn how to think, then the information that goes in may never come back out."* I'd add *we need graduates that have the determination to finish a task that takes a period of time to do. We need students who have inquisitiveness, courage to stand alone, honesty, diligence... so they can do something with the information they have access to.*

I'm not saying academics are unimportant. By no means! A base of knowledge makes it easier for a person to learn even more. However, we must not only teach our children facts, but how to find and use them. To knowledge, add understanding and to understanding, wisdom.

How does this affect our methods of teaching? How do people actually learn best? Not only how do they retain information but more importantly, how do they learn to reason, to think, to *do* something with all that information?

We tend to teach as we were taught, at least until we have a clear vision of a better alternative. So what is that alternative? Well, to begin with, we should study fewer topics, but study them in depth. We should teach the basics well, but we should also teach our children to think. Here's how.

Take a theme and develop it deeply over a period of several weeks. Your child will learn how to get information and what to do with that information once he has it. You're preparing him for life in the real world!

The average elementary science textbook claims to cover everything from plants and animals, to our solar system, to energy and machines, to weather, and rocks and minerals in one year. *Impossible!* And that's just the science book. This may look great on a scope and sequence chart, but a closer look will show you that topics are only partially covered, perhaps even just mentioned.

Thankfully, homeschool educators are not limited to what some bureaucracy says must be *"covered in a given school year."* Children do not have to study a certain topic, for example, the solar system in the third grade. So the children in your family, whatever their ages, can all study the solar system in the same year. You decide what's best for your own situation.

More and more homeschools are depending less on copying the styles of classrooms and are instead developing a style of teaching that is unique to our home school movement. Your family explores and learns together about a single topic (birds, weather, WWII.) You probe every fascinating question that pops up until you're "experts" on the topic. In educational jargon, this is called *unit studies.* (Many in the educational establishment also recognize the unit study approach is the best way to teach. It's just not so easy with 20-plus pupils!)

Take your Time!
Do you know how long our family spent on the two explorers, Magellan and Marco Polo in our homeschool? (This is an extreme example.) We spent twelve weeks on just those two explorers. We could have spent longer but it was time to move on.

Magellan sailed all the way around the world. There's a lot to learn about the whole world that Magellan saw. And what about his men? What were they like? What happened on his voyage? Did they like Magellan? Was he easy to get along with? What did Magellan believe about God? Did he make any discoveries along the way? Did he meet any new peoples? What were they like? How did they dress? Can we make some costumes like they wore? What sort of ship did he travel on? How did they know how to navigate? Can we learn to navigate by the stars, too? What else can we learn about the stars?

How do we know what Magellan's travels were like? Did he keep a diary? Can we also keep a diary? What was it like sleeping under the stars on a ship? Can we also sleep under the stars, perhaps on some wooden planks to get the full effect? What did they eat on the ship? Can we eat that too? How about if we eat it over a period of days to get the real idea? What was scurvy? How did they prevent it? Why? What are vitamins? *And on and on...*

Can you see how deep it is possible to go into a topic? Will we remember Magellan? Will we learn anything else along the way?

This may seem a little much for some of us couch potatoes who'd rather sit passively watching TV rather than pursue a good book or new hobby. Advertisers say our attention spans are shorter than ever. *We tune out quickly so give it to us fast before you lose us.*

BIRD BINGE

Our family studied a unit about birds together for one month. At the time we had three children, ages 3-10. During the week we snuggled on the sofa, reading about the characteristics of birds, looking at diagrams of body parts of birds, and learning about the various places birds can live.

A natural outgrowth of our reading was a desire to see birds firsthand. At the hardware store we saw a birdfeeder that would attach to a window of our home. We bought it and filled it with seed. Overnight, our backyard was transformed into a winter sanctuary where cardinals, jays, finches, nuthatches, and sparrows feasted.

A friend at our church heard of our study and invited us to her backyard pond to see the Canada geese residing for the winter. While there, we found lovely large quill feathers. We took them home for a closer observation using a magnifying glass. A few of these quill feathers became quill pens after we shaped them into writing tools to be dipped into ink.

Meanwhile, we read everything we could get our hands on about birds. Our family invested in an Audubon Society handbook for identifying birds we would see on walks or from our window.

During this same month, I had an interesting phone call. My mother-in-law told me of someone she called the "Audubon Lady". It seems that in our town was an active group of bird lovers with a leader. I called the "Audubon Lady" and she invited us to her home. There she gave the girls and me a whole morning of instruction about birds, their habits, identification, and to top it all off, she loaned us a set of recorded tapes with authentic bird calls. We could now begin to identify unseen birds by their calls. (God arranges these coincidences for homeschoolers all the time.)

One Sunday afternoon near the end of our bird unit, we invited our grandparents for a "bird day". I set up learning stations around the house and paired one adult with each child. The adult/child teams circulated around the house, spending 20 minutes at each learning station. One station had reference books where the team was to match beaks and feet with pictures of birds, deducting what birds might eat based on the shape of their beaks. Another station had books with paintings by John James Audubon. The pair tried watercoloring. At a third station, the team made simple bird feeders. What was I doing the whole time? I was in the kitchen preparing dinner while the grandparents did a week's worth of home teaching activity for me!

We don't take time to smell the roses or watch a sunset anymore. We don't take time to watch a squirrel hide an acorn... or find it. Lack of time saps our curiosity and our lack of curiosity saps our stick-to-it-ive-ness. Homeschooling is flexible enough to accommodate a more fruitful approach to learning. *Creativity and curiosity are ignited as we allow our children the time to figure things out, to discover for themselves without rushing.*

Real-life Learning

If you need to learn about something, perhaps either for work or related to a special interest of yours, how do you do it? (Stop for a minute and really think about your answer.)

I've asked this question in seminars before and I usually get answers like *"Go to the library. Read a magazine article. Learn about the subject with videos. Try to talk to a person who knows the subject and has done it."* Eventually you try it yourself. You might even refer to a textbook, as a last resort!

Just suppose you were personally interested in learning to forecast the weather. I doubt seriously if the first place you'd go would be a science textbook to learn weather forecasting.

For one thing, a science textbook probably wouldn't have a complete section on weather forecasting. It might have a brief overview; it might tell about some instruments but not others. Or, it might have four or five pages of highly condensed information where someone new to the subject needs more explanation. You don't want to be hit with 15 new words on four or five pages. You need some time to understand the vocabulary involved in weather forecasting because it is new to you.

Instead, you might talk to a friend who knows weather forecasting, or you might go to the librarian to ask for help finding information. I'll bet you wouldn't care whether the librarian directed you to a book that is exactly on your reading grade level or not, either. If anything, you'd probably hope she directed you to a book a little below your reading level since this subject is new to you. (*Remember that, home teachers.*)

While you're there, you might become interested in reading a biography of a famous amateur weather forecaster like Louis Reuben. If you were really interested in forecasting the weather you wouldn't want to just read about it — you'd want to try it! You'd want to experiment with weather forecasting yourself.

Textbooks are only a fraction of the way we learn. In homeschool, don't rely on them as your main source of information.

Why not? There are many reasons. Especially on the elementary level, textbooks skim the subject area. I laugh when I remember

DOUBTING DADS

Dads often ask me, "How do children who use the unit approach do on standardized tests and what if we leave something out?" Let me answer that question with a true life illustration.

Last year Katie (not her real name), age 13, took standardized tests in social studies and science. Her mother wanted to see how she compared with other children who had completed grade eight since she would be entering high school this year. Katie was a little put out with her mother for making her take a test that was not required by state law. "Besides," she said, "you haven't finished teaching me history!" "We've only gotten through the constitutional period!," she reminded her mother. "We haven't even done the Civil War, yet! And we've never even used a science book."

"Yes," her mother said, "but you've learned more than you realize in those unit studies. Let's just see how you compare to others." Had her mother left something out? I suppose you could say she had since she had not gotten to any American history beyond the birth of our nation! With some fear, Katie took the test. Her scores? 98th percentile on the history test; 99th percentile on the science. When asked what she thought of the dreaded history test, Katie replied, "Really, all you had to know how to do was read."

Do you want to help your child prepare for standardized testing? Give him the language tools to read and understand new content. Ask your child questions that require thinking, perhaps even over a period of days. Wait for the answer. Standardized tests do not measure factual data, but rather they measure reading and interpretation skills.

Standardized tests are designed to measure achievement of students in many and varied curriculums across the nation. The children in Texas do not have the same subjects in the same grade as the children in Virginia.

Sequence is not important in unit studies as it is in the foundational basics, (reading, writing and arithmetic.) One state may study insects in grade three, a second state in grade six and a third not at all. Unit topics need not follow a certain sequence in order for your children to do well on standardized tests.

Your children don't have to do certain things in certain grades in order to keep up with the schools. Besides, there is too much information available now to limit it to a given set of facts that we all must learn. Your children are not expected to know every item on any nationally standardized achievement test. Teach children the learning and thinking process. Children who learn this way will do well on standardized tests.

the social studies textbooks that were used when I was in school. (At least those books were centered on real social studies — history and geography and not what we have today—socialism, population control, and one world government. But that's beside the point.)

Each year those textbooks began with one sentence or paragraph about each explorer. Each year I memorized the same facts for the first history test and promptly forgot the information afterwards. Never did I learn the types of things I learned with my girls about Magellan. It wasn't very interesting, either. Textbooks were like a Reader's Digest condensed version with too many chapters left out.

If you use textbooks as your sole source of information what are you teaching your child about how to learn? Will he develop a realistic view of real-life learning? Or will he think he knows it all after reading a textbook account and passing a test?

Some children equate education with reading a chapter, studying for a test, regurgitating the information, and promptly forgetting it because it was useless anyway. Some children think education ends with filling in the blanks to pass a grade. Learning can be fun! It's fun to study explorers if you get to sleep all night on a wooden plank under the stars and eat hardtack you made yourself without a cookbook. (Explorers didn't carry cookbooks along!)

There is a danger in thinking a subject has been covered if a textbook has been read and a test passed. When I did annual achievement testing of homeschooled children, I saw too many children who had studied under a workbook approach to history or science who could not apply what they had learned on standardized tests. Material was memorized and soon forgotten. Their parents would tell me the children read the workbooks, answered all the questions and did wonderfully on chapter tests. (What happened between the time the subject was studied and the yearly achievement test was given? Could it be that the information was meaningless to the child and discarded along the way?)

Textbooks often present difficult material in a highly condensed fashion. New vocabulary words are met only a few times, but retention is expected. On the other hand, if information is given in what I call a *real* book — a library book — that same vocabulary may be met over and over again. Retention is naturally better since the word is met more times. Therefore, use a good quality high school textbook as a reference resource for an outline if you wish, but rely on *real* books for information.

Why do we even have textbooks then, if they are so inefficient in presenting subject matter? Why were they even designed? They were designed for convenience in teaching a large group at once.

UNIT STUDY ADVANTAGES

All ages learn together — a great recipe for family togetherness!
(Use your ideas when the grandparents visit, for party themes, etc.).

Learning becomes a natural way of life.

Generates curiosity and independent thinking in children.

We are not constrained by artificial time constraints.

Planning time is reduced — Fewer "subjects" are taught at one time, simplifying your life as a mother/teacher.

Learning becomes meaningful when interrelated—
Retention is improved. Children remember what they study deeply!

Gives a realistic approach to learning and prepares the child for lifetime learning — Thinking rather than memorization is taught.

You can do it! You don't have to know it all; learn with your children.

While high school texts do make nice reference books for us, we are not trying to imitate a classroom in our home.

Why am I picking on textbooks? Because, as homeschoolers, we are so dependent on them. Afraid to let them go. Too many parents try to use both textbooks and the unit approach to teaching, practically wiping out both themselves and their children because they were afraid to let the textbooks go... just in case.

Advantages of the unit approach

Since all ages learn together *you have a great recipe for family togetherness.* You teach the same material to all the children at once. This is handy for those of you who're schooling several children. You may have a 12-year-old, a 9-year-old, and a 5-year-old all learning about the explorers at the same time. Simply adjust independent assignments according to the abilities of each child.

For example, the 12-year-old might be reading a biography about a particular explorer of interest. She can present her findings to the rest of the family. The 9-year-old may be writing in her diary each day. The 5-year-old may be dressing up and role-playing what you've been reading to the family aloud.

When we studied the Revolutionary War, my 3-year-old dressed like Abigail Adams for one month straight. She role-played what we had been reading aloud in a biography of Abigail Adams over and over each day. My 10-year-old drew a map siting the battles of the war, and together we planned a tea in the British / Boston tradition and invited grandmother. I read aloud **Johnny Tremain** after which we all watched the video.

Break large subjects into smaller research topics for individual children to share with the family. For example, when we were studying plants and animals, our daughter, Amy (12), researched tropical rainforests. After writing a short research paper, she reported to us about the delicately balanced ecosystem in the rainforests of Brazil today. Daughter, Heather (8) read a delightful book called **Rabbit Spring** which told in beautiful story form of the life of rabbits and hares. Orally, she shared her findings with the whole family. Meg (4) and Britt (2) found and captured huge beetles under our woodpile in the backyard. They caught them with their killing jars, mounted them with the help of older sisters, and then shared with the family what they had learned about the living quarters of black wood beetles. (*"What were they eating? How many were there? Did they like it when you exposed them to sunlight?..."*)

The whole family learns and interacts together! Isn't that what homeschooling is all about?

Learning becomes a way of life.
Some of our best learning times have taken place outside of so-called school hours. As we gradually get away from the notion that school must be paper and books and desks, we find learning is a natural part of our lives as a family. Suddenly it feels easy.

When we travel, I try to find a book or literature related to the area we are visiting. It was great fun reading the **Jack Tales** while passing through southwest Virginia last spring. When our family visited the coast of North Carolina this summer, I read aloud about the pirates of the 1700's. Blackbeard really came to life!

Use days with grandparents to set up centers related to the unit you're studying — Watch them teach the children for you! A week's worth of activity can be accomplished in one afternoon.

Family nights with other homeschoolers can accomplish the same thing. With Dads present your teaching time can be cut in half and it is motivational for the children.

Integrated learning generates curiosity and critical thinking
Expect to have a learning adventure with your child. We're not raising sheep. We want our children involved in learning rather than just passively receiving and reiterating information. *"You figure it out for yourself"* is as important a response to our children's questions as just giving the answer. Our present society of school-aged children needs a heavy dose of *"You figure it out."*

By the way, figuring it out takes more time than just memorizing and regurgitating answers. That's okay... we have the time. As you've noticed by now, *we are not limited by time constraints.* If we are involved in a project, that project can last for hours or even days if we like because we don't have to meet the P.E. teacher for 25 minutes at 1:03 p.m..

Planning Time is reduced. Instead of planning dozens of topics in various history and science textbooks, you concentrate on one theme and do it well. On the other hand, if you had three children in three different science and history textbooks, you could be planning nine topics at once. (Think how long it would take!) In that situation, your textbook too easily becomes your sole source of information.

Learning is more meaningful.
As you study one topic at a time you can interrelate all the disciplines around that topic. For example if you are studying the explorers, you interrelate art, geography and science, all around those explorers. If you are studying Marco Polo's travels, you might have an opportunity to learn silk screening because that is something he saw in his travels to the east. You'll have plenty of

opportunity to learn geography as you map the routes the explorers took. Science could be raising silkworms because Marco Polo discovered silk in China. Learning is meaningful to children when it's connected. Children remember what they study this way.

Unit Studies prepares your child for life-long learning.
You are giving your child the skill to retrieve and organize information. Real books are used, not just textbooks followed by tests. The purpose of learning is not to put a correct answer on a piece of paper. Remember how *you* study a topic *you* are interested in? We want our children to become lifelong learners. To learn how to learn in real life.

You can do it! Fortunately, you don't have to know it all! You learn with your children. There is not one right way to do your unit study. You know what is best for your children. You will not know everything before you start. When we began studying birds, I knew what a cardinal looked like and not much more! When we studied the human eye, together we watched a video series to learn how to dissect a cow's eyeball before we tried it ourselves. As you learn together, trust yourself to make decisions that are right for your family.

Your investment?
There's a flip side to every coin. Teaching this way takes some effort. *You must make choices for yourself.* How much time will you spend in an area? What will be the direction of your units? What books will you choose to read? Which activities will you pursue? Most of us are afraid of making wrong choices.

Relax. Learn how to learn with your children. Forget about mastering mounds of workbooks. Take a broad rather than narrow view of education. Workbooks are written on a mentally low level (read and regurgitate). A whole world is waiting to be discovered.

Involving your child in hands-on learning requires energy from you. Hands-on learning develops logical thinking and problem-solving, but you will need to provide supplies and there will be clean-up. A house where children are involved in projects is not always neat.

WHAT TO INCLUDE IN A UNIT STUDY

Vocabulary. Select words related to the topic.
          (Short lists are best.)

Writing:
   preschoolers- collage picture reports
   primary- oral reports using pictures, charts, etc.
   elementary- short written reports,
               learn to use notecards for oral presentations,
   middle school/high school- longer reports,
               research papers using several references.

Oral reports

Reading related to the unit
   library resource books, fiction and non-fiction,
   maps, charts

Hands-on experience with the topic

Art, music, literature related to the topic

Bible (memory, application, word study, cross reference study)

Practical life application (ex. learn to predict weather by looking
      at cloud formations, or learn how to build and maintain a
      compost pile when studying plants.)

Field trips

What do we include in unit studies?

Whether you learn about inventions or ancient Egypt, you, the teacher, interrelate all disciplines around that topic. Consider our family's bird study. We researched the characteristics of birds (*science*), we observed Audubon's paintings and tried to paint ourselves (*art*), we visited the "Audubon Lady" and my friend's pond (*field trip*), we wrote thank you's to both wonderful women (*language arts*), we read **The Ugly Duckling** by Hans Christian Andersen (*literature*), we read a biography of John James Audubon (*history*), and so on. As one thought leads to another, your child wants to find out more and develop projects and reading interests of his own.

Vocabulary is crucial to your unit study as it establishes a base of knowledge that makes it possible to learn even more. Master the vocabulary of a subject and you understand that subject.

You'll have many opportunities for writing, whether about a field trip, about a recipe you tried, or reporting as if you were an eye witness in a news account. But give as many opportunities as possible for hands-on experience via field trips and doing when studying these units too. Isn't it better to raise silkworms yourself than just read about it in a textbook?

What about chronological teaching? Before high school, lots of experience is important but chronological order is not. Young children do not view time the way we do. When you are an adult, chronological study begins to make sense. In the meantime, use a large timeline, posted on the wall, to tie together the pieces of history you study. Get to know historical figures before learning survey course facts. Save survey courses for high school. (See *What's Included in Science* and *What's Included in Social Studies* pages for recommended survey courses.)

Assessing Unit Study Curriculum Choices

You may wish to prepare your own unit studies, branching into subject areas as desired. *Not feeling so creative? Just want to save time?* Select a prepared unit study curriculum.

Choose one that will produce thinkers. Does the program just *tell* the information? Don't use it. Choose one that encourages the child to find out for himself as much as possible.

Are there enough ideas for you to choose from? Remember your child is unique and you want to have choices that will fit your situation.

Is it flexible? If your family gets the flu for one week will you have guilt attacks because you didn't do every listed activity?

Is it creative? Will it be fun for you and the children? Does it stretch your imagination as a teacher? Can you branch away from it on rabbit trails your family chooses to follow?

Record-keeping

How do you hold the pieces of a unit study together? Since you're not using a textbook, where will you keep all the information?

Have the child record what he is learning in his 3-ring binder. On one day he might write a summary of information he read that day. The next day he might write an eye-witness news account of what he saw in Magellan's travels. He might write about a field trip to the art museum to see samples of silks and Persian rugs like those that Marco Polo would have seen in his travels, or diagram the explorers' journeys on a map. Binders are an convenient way to collect information.

Record unit topics studied on the **Curriculum Scope Chart** included in the organizational section of this manual. Remember to keep one chart per child for easy reference. *"Have I done the American Revolution with Heather? How old was she?"*

What about Social Studies and Science?

Okay, you've decided to use the unit study approach in your home-school. You've given up your crutch. That crutch is what the curriculum planners have told you that you should be teaching each year in a given subject area. Now what do you do? What if you leave something out? Let's look briefly at what is included in social studies and science and see how to teach these subjects.

Social Studies

Curriculum planners don't have a magic formula that says, *"In the first grade, you are to study firemen and rescue workers... In the sixth grade, you are to study the Far East and South America... etc."* There's no such thing. Truth is, it doesn't matter which order you choose. The order you choose will not affect your children's achievement test scores. It's also not important to their scores that you cover every possible topic taught by every teacher in every school. Cover fewer areas deeply.

So what's included in social studies? When we say social studies, we're referring to history, geography, government, good citizenship, and economics. Undoubtedly, home educators have the best possible avenue for teaching citizenship and economics. We can involve our children in work and service projects. We can involve our children in learning about government as we read current events with them or as we keep them up to date on laws and issues that are being discussed in our general assemblies and in congress. This is *living* social studies.

Integrate social studies with art, music, and literature. The arts, music, and literature are the best communicators of our past!

Reading, vocabulary, and even spelling assignments should be drawn from the unit you're studying. Whatever topic you choose, cover it well using all subject areas.

For the very young child, start your study of social studies by explaining your family's roots. Young children also benefit greatly from role playing men and women from our past whom the older children are studying.

Remember that 3-year-old who role-played Abigail Adams for a semester? She woke up each morning, dressed in her costume, and carried her diary and bayberry candles around all day. (It was great for the laundry load since Abigail Adams didn't wash clothes often at all.) Along the same line, relate geography to the people in foreign places. Children identify with children of other lands.

WHAT'S INCLUDED IN
Social Studies

Friends & Neighbors

neighborhoods
urban / suburban / rural
city / town / county / state
dairy
greenhouse
bakers
stores, etc.

Children in other lands

homes
folk customs
families

Geography

globe, map skills
climate regions
topography
natural resources

History

early civilizations
ancient empires
Middle Ages
European Renaissance & Reformation
rise of European nations

national heroes
world heros
our presidents
explorers

national holidays
local, state
American Indians

colonists
Revolutionary period
Constitution
our government
pioneers - westward movement
Civil War

industrial growth
World Wars
present day

High School Survey Courses
World Geography
World History
American History
Government
Economics

Use a timeline as a framework for collecting bits of historical knowledge as it is learned. Did you notice the phrase "as it is learned"? Don't expect your children to learn a lot from a pre-printed timeline. Just post characters on the timeline as they are studied.

Even a 2-year-old learns from a timeline by seeing the big picture of time. But don't post too many characters at once. And be sure the ones you use are meaningful to your children. Keep your timeline simple for clarity.

(**What's Included in Social Studies** lists topics usually covered in social studies for grades kindergarten through high school. Use these for selecting units you want to study. Stay on a subject as long as it is interesting to you and the children. One topic leads to another, so just use this list as a starting point.)

Science

Science is part of unit studies as well. Again, rather than impart information about a series of topics in science, choose a few topics to cover thoroughly.

There are two levels of learning in science. One is the *information level.* The other is the *process level.* If you want to develop a true scientist, have that child involved in the process, the *doing* of science, rather than just in the accumulation of knowledge. Once your child has experienced science he will want to get the information. Science was never meant to be only a collection of facts, memorization, and regurgitation for a test. Instead, it includes asking questions, researching, observing, discovering, measuring, and using scientific discovery. (Our friend Mr. Jefferson understood this quite well.)

Do as many experiments together as possible. Many books are available that give experiments using items found readily in your home. Look for these! You'll have fun! Use a high school science textbook for reference and go with the interest of your child. Science supplies are readily available. Start by ordering the catalogs listed in the appendix.

Gradually build a laboratory in your home. Our kitchens are natural laboratories. We don't need bunsen burners, we have a stovetop. The sink is handy and since our children don't have 25 other children to contend with, they can do each and every science experiment themselves. They won't have to sit by watching the teacher do it! And stay alert for spiritual lessons that are always there in science, too.

WHAT'S INCLUDED IN **Science**

Being a Scientist

The Scientific Method

classification
observation
prediction
interpretation

theories, assumptions, limitations

discoveries
great scientists

metric measurement

careers
scientific ethics

Animals
birds / mammals
amphibians / reptiles / fish
insects / life cycle / collections
environments

Humans
nutrition
body systems / organs

Microscopic
cells
bacteria
molds / algae / fungi

Plants
flowers / seeds / bulbs
reproduction
trees

Universe
sun / moon / planets
constellations

Earth
gravity
volcanoes / earthquakes
rocks / soils / minerals / fossils
weather / air masses, fronts
seasons / time
day / night
atmosphere / air pressure
air / water / climate
oceanography
ecology

Chemistry
heat / temperature
chemical changes
molecules / elements
compounds / mixtures
lots of experiments

Energy
atoms / nuclear power
conservation / fuels
magnetism / electricity

Technology
machines
simple motors / engines
transportation
electronics
inventions / inventors

High School Survey Courses
Earth Science • Biology • Chemistry • Physics

The process skills

Science is not only memorizing information. It involves learning by doing. The first skill is *observation*. Let's say you are doing an experiment with beans. You have planted the beans and you are observing growth over a period of days. You might have the child measure the growth as part of the observation of those bean shoots.

For *interpretation*, you may have the child do something to the beans prior to the planting, say, expose some of the beans to the microwave or soak some of the beans overnight in hot water. Then observe the growth, measure, and interpret what happened to the beans based on what was done to them prior to planting.

With the same experience, you could *classify* information. Suppose you have several beans that were zapped in the microwave, several that were soaked, and several with nothing done to them (the control group). Suppose you organize data that is collected. That way you can make some comparisons.

If you want to *record* in writing what happened in the experiment, that's communication. Use numbers often to express the information.

Next, the child can *predict*. He can make theories about what will happen in a future experiment or about what will happen if a different function were performed on the beans before planting. Then he could *test* his theory to see if his prediction really happens.

These are all process skills. Choose science activities that include process skills. You want your child to *discover* science. You won't always tell him what he is supposed to think!

(On the opposite page I have given you an overview of what's included in science. Don't think you have to cover everything listed. Use this page for ideas. This is a compilation of topics covered in various school curriculums across our nation in kindergarten-high school.)

The Big Picture

Why have I stressed the unit approach so strongly? Not only do children learn best this way, but there is also a bigger picture.

Ours is a society that spends, on the average, as much time in front of a television as at work. We have become intellectually lazy. We're intimidated by information — overwhelmed by the constant flood of new data.

Television programmers tell us the average adult's attention span is ten minutes. We want specialized information given to us in an organized fashion. Preferably in small bite-size pieces. (Why do you think politicians have learned to speak in "sound-bites?") We want to be told what that information means, too often even what to think!

The young people who learn to think, to discern truth from fiction, to retrieve, organize and communicate pertinent information will be the adults who will impact our society in the future.

Can you see the big picture of education now? Can you see what God can do with Christian men and women, our next generation, who can interpret data and communicate that information? Can God use *your* child in the big picture?

So, plan ahead for learning and exploring together. Your youngsters will love becoming experts. And who knows? — Our home-school generation may be God's special servants in training!

Notes:

In this chapter...

- ## Real-life math

- ## Training problem-solvers

Rev. 920

Section Three, Chapter Two

Math —
The Homeschool
Advantage

*The primary goal is to be able to apply math to
daily life and on the job, to solve real-life problems.*

You won't fail in teaching math!

How can I say that? Because I've seen hundreds of parents
succeed. All it takes is understanding the basics and mixing
that understanding with love and patience.

Everything we've discussed so far about learning applies to math
— teaching at each child's level, taking their unique personalities
into account, focusing on real-life applications, learning by doing,
teaching our children to be problem-solvers, etc.

For example, whenever we teach, whether it is reading, written
language, or math, we should be goal oriented. So what's the
point of teaching math?

The point is not to teach facts or rules, though both must be
mastered for efficiency in math. The point is to be able to use
math in daily life and on the job to solve real life problems.

To do this, the child must be able to think mathematically.
He learns to see the orderliness of our number system and relationships between numbers. And he sees how math is used in
our daily lives.

There are a number of fine books on teaching mathematics
(some fairly exhaustive); we won't duplicate those here. We will
look at examples of how to help your child discover the intrigue of
thinking with numbers, and how that understanding develops.

And you won't need to have a Ph.D. in mathematics either!

16

Real-life Learning from Math

How am I supposed to teach a child to think mathematically? Well, there are two basic approaches. One emphasizes memorizing facts and filling in workbook pages. The other emphasizes using objects, games and examples from real-life to make the concepts concrete for the young learner.

You may have guessed that I favor the second approach. But just how do we pull it off? Here's an example.

Let's create a large 100 chart to show your child the relationships in our number system. Construct a large number poster. Make 100 squares on the poster approximately one inch square each. Put one numeral in each square, 1-100. Arrange the numerals in rows of 10 each. Do you get the picture?

Now, what relationships can you see between the numbers? Take a problem such as 3 + 4. Have the child point to three on the chart. Then take four jumps. Where does the child land? The child lands on the number 7, showing 3 + 4 equals 7. (Or, you can show subtraction by hopping backwards.) You can show 9 x 3 = 27 by saying, *"Show me 9. Now count 9 more... Now 9 more. Where do you land?"* Or, 27 divided by 3. *"Start at the 27. How many times can you jump backwards 3 before using all 27?"* As you show your child how to count by 3's, 5's, 2's, or 10's using hops on the chart, he develops a mental map of our number system.

If your child is still young enough, he may need something concrete to help keep his place. If so, have him put buttons or beans in the squares to demonstrate the problem. (By the way, what you and I may call *beans*, sophisticated educators refer to as *manipulatives*.) If you prefer not to make your own chart, you can buy one at practically any bookfair, or teacher supply store. Keep your eyes open!

That's just one tool to use with your child to demonstrate relationships between numbers and the inherent orderliness in mathematics. Your child will be thrilled as he discovers math's logic!

Along the same line as the earlier 100 chart, have your child later write the numerals 1-100 in vertical columns to see the relationships. The twist of course is the *vertical* columns by 10's. Let them play the same games on this chart as on the first. *Look Mom! These numbers work the same way!*

Here's another concrete tool. (In fact, this is the best concrete tool you can have in your kit!) Construct or buy a cube kit to teach place value and addition/subtraction/multiplication/division. Use single cubes for the ones, a bar of 10 cubes for the 10's and squares of ten 10 bars for the hundreds. (Guess what the thousand cube looks like?) Using these 1's cubes, 10's bars, 100's squares and

Rev. 9201

1,000's cubes, you can do all sorts of arithmetic like borrowing and carrying (regrouping), and easily see place value of large numbers. (If you're not brave enough to make your own kit, wooden cube sets constructed of fine hardwood are available.)

You will want to play lots of board games, games in which you must count moves, use money, use a spinner, keep score, etc.. Show your kids how to match dominoes. Games force your child to think mathematically without even realizing it!

Let your child play with a hand held calculator. Have him punch in the numbers you call or a sequence of numbers that you call. Learn to skip count forward and backward as perparation for multiplying and dividing.

You can find all sorts of math brain teasers in books in your junior library. For fun, do these puzzles and teasers together. Do mental math drill in the car. *"5 + 5 x 6 divided by 12 equals what?"* For thought questions, force the child to think of solutions for extended periods, even overnight before giving an answer. Don't allow quick, thoughtless answers. The child who plays games that require math and who does math brain teasers and puzzles with you will begin to think mathematically!

By the way, be sure when you purchase a prepared curriculum that it gives you lots of concrete teaching activities to use. Then add your own ideas and games.

Everyday Math

So, numbers intrigue us and math is fun. But how do we get our children to see the usefulness of math? Include the child in daily mathematical decisions you are making. When you go to the bank, explain to that child how to use a checkbook or how to keep records and accounts. When you are baking a cake, explain how to read the directions in the cookbook, how to measure, how to double a recipe for a crowd. Encourage your child to participate in mathematical thinking throughout the day.

"The four of you are going to the movies together and each ticket costs $3.50. How much will it cost?" Have him figure it out before he goes to the ticket window. *"We have 12 M&Ms left in the candy dish."* How many does each child get? Even a toddler can do that one accurately if you give him plenty of time to discover the answer on his own. They'll even do remainders!

When you choose a math curriculum, be sure to choose one that supports your focus on learning concepts and doesn't rely totally on drill or repetition. Choose one that balances the two. And don't overlook those teacher's manuals. They teach you how to present concepts to your child. Workbooks should be only a part of the total math picture. Choose a curriculum that includes thinking and discovery— you must not just teach the child *how* but *why* when you do math.

Am I saying it's not important to memorize the facts? Far from it. A child must memorize the facts to go on to more complicated problem solving. He must have the facts at his fingertips. Balance drill and concept!

Math Readiness

As with language skills, the preschool years are the best time to lay a foundation of experiences that will make learning later concepts that much more natural. There are four basic areas of math readiness that will develop naturally as your child spends time with you at home. What are they?

1. *One corresponds to one.* Picture a dinner table. When you set a table there is one place per seat, one plate per seat, one fork per seat, one glass, and so on. Even at Sunday dinner, the child learns that one corresponds to one. Another way to teach him that one corresponds to one is to let him make a tally mark on a chalk board or piece of paper each time you clap your hands or someone drops a clothespin into a jar or throws a beanbag into a can.

Use games for fun, and to hold interest. When you play musical chairs, you are teaching one to one correspondence. Draw dots on paper and have the child match pennies or beans to the certain number of dots.

Ask your child numerical questions which he or she can answer using beans or popsicle sticks or those cute little toy people. For example, *"How many people are in our family?"* Have them put down one bean or stick for each person in the family. *"Well, what if we invite grandmother and grandfather? How many people will there be then?"* As the child uses the beans, the one-to-one concept sinks in deeper and deeper. In fact, for most of us, all four basic concepts are so ingrained that they seem intuitive common sense.

2. *Alike/Different.* By differences, I mean differences in sizes, amounts, and shapes. For example, have your child match the various sizes (diameters) of plates or glasses to shapes you have drawn on a large sheet of paper. The child sees that one glass has a wide diameter and matches the wide circle you drew. Another glass was more narrow and matches the small shape.

Another way to see similarities and differences in shapes is to have your child find all the triangles, circles, squares, or hexagons in a given room, store, or parking lot. Don't stop with the simple shapes. Move on to advanced shapes when he is ready.

Rev. 9201

Teach differences using connecting cubes to measure a length of string or length of pencil or a length of straw. Have the child measure body parts using the connecting cubes. How many connnecting cubes long is Daddy's nose? Is his nose longer or shorter than Mom's? Or, use the string to measure. Then to extend the activity, measure the string against a ruler to see how many centimeters or inches long Daddy's nose is.

Fit lids to variously sized containers. Make and use your own jigsaw puzzles using magazine pictures pasted on cardboard.

3. *Sets.* For example, group 3 beans in one little neat pile and 4 beans in another little neat pile. See the two sets. Make sets with buttons or beads. Organize sets not only according to how many but according to color. *"Can you put all the yellow buttons in one pile and the white buttons in another? Or make one set with all the large buttons and one set with all the small buttons? Which set of buttons has more?"* or *"Group all the nails in one pile and the screws in another."* or *"Group all the pennies in one pile and the nickels in another."* Can your child think of other ways to group the sets? (Can he group sets of toys in his closet?)

Playing dominoes also demonstrates sets to the child. *" There are two sets on each domino, one on each half of the domino. How many do we get when the two sets are combined? What if we cover one half of the domino? How many dots are left?"*

Cut up egg cartons to show sets. Then regroup those sets to show 12 or one dozen again. Or divide raisins equally among children.

4. *Counting.* When you teach your child to count, be sure he counts slowly in order to see one-to-one correspondence. When you are counting objects, have the child touch the item, say the number, touch the item, say the next number, and so on. He takes the raisin, counts it, puts it down. Takes the raisin, counts it, puts it down in an orderly fashion so he doesn't lose track. The two year old will typically count 1, 2, 3, 4, 5,...quickly and skim through them. Have the child practice counting in the grocery store as he picks out 6 good apples for the bag or 3 perfect lemons.

During this readiness period, emphasize games and let your young child move while he is learning. Ideas are endless. He can jump four times after you have clapped four times. Or hop up the steps the correct number of times. This movement will keep his interest because he is involved in learning.

Don't forget to deliberately seek out manipulatives for hands-on learning. Research and your own good sense tell you a young child does better with something concrete he can handle.

MATH READINESS

Use what naturally occurs in your home for teaching. Emphasize games and activity! Ideas are endless—here are a few to get you started.

ONE CORRESPONDS TO ONE
- Set the table—one fork per plate, one napkin per plate, etc.

- Make a tally mark each time a bell is rung or your hands clap.

- Match pennies to a number of dots drawn on paper.

- Ask numerical questions the child can answer with beads, buttons, (example-how many chairs at the table, people in our family, etc.)

SAME/DIFFERENT
- Match variously sized glasses, plates, etc., to shapes drawn by you on paper.

- Find all circles, triangles, squares, rectangles, hexagons, etc., in a room, parking lot, store, etc.

- Fit lids to variously sized containers.

- Make and use jigsaw puzzles.

- Measure parts of the body, objects in a room, with string.

SETS
- Sort objects such as beans, buttons, beads
    — by color, size or shape
    — according to two categories like color *and* size
      (*"all the large, blue buttons together."*)

- Use dominoes, beans, egg cartons to show a number.
  (*"How many ways can you make two groups add up to 10?"*)

- Have children divide cookies or M&Ms equally among them.

COUNTING
- Be sure the child counts s-l-o-w-l-y to see one-to-one concept.

- Count fruit as he puts it into the bag at the grocery store.

- Jump/hop four times after you clap four times.

Rev. 920

Elementary Math

In this stage, there are two basic skills to master — *computation* and *problem solving*.

Computation

Computation is the obvious in math. The goal of calculation is to be able to solve problems both accurately and rapidly. If your child is still counting on fingers or even verbalizing as he computes, he is not ready for very advanced problem solving. Good computational skills are prerequisite to problem solving. Work on this with drills such as flashcards, listening to tables on tape, oral recitation, copying on board or paper, games, dominoes, or math bingo.

In computation, we must teach *place value* so that our children can borrow and carry (also known as regrouping). We teach the *basic math* functions (addition, subtraction, multiplication, and division), *fractions*, *time* (and how to use the time throughout the day), and *money* (how to use real money and how to calculate money). We've succeeded with computation when these are just as natural as *one-to-one* or *alike/different*.

Place Values

Remember the cube sets I mentioned a few pages ago? This kit is a tremendous tool for teaching place value. You'll find that you use it over and over because it is 3-dimensional and not 2-dimensional. You see, those little pictures in the workbook that depict place value might be enough for you, an adult, but children understand place value much more clearly by playing hands-on with the concept. A kit like this can serve you through at least grades 3 or 4.

Fractions

Be sure to start with the concrete to teach fractions as well. Little printed "pie" circles in your child's workbook aren't concrete. Concrete is something you can hold and move in your hand.

One way to teach fractions is right in the kitchen. When you measure, taking a fourth of a cup of this and a half teaspoon of that, you are using fractions. Your child can learn fractions right beside you. Use a real pie, not just a pie printed in a book. (Later, you can make pie slices from felt for lots of use.)

Give problems with fractions. *"Our family ate one half of the pie today. If we eat one half of what is left for lunch tomorrow, what fraction of the pie will be left?"* Give your child a real pie and I guarantee he'll figure that one out!

ELEMENTARY MATH

COMPUTATIONAL SKILLS:

Place value
Use base ten blocks and cubes for a concrete manipulative.

Addition, subtraction, multiplication, division

Fractions:
Start with concrete examples, show how to make halves, fourths, eighths, using felt cut-outs, paper plates, etc.

Time:
Use a real clock with moveable hands.

Set clock for times certain things are done.

Use time throughout the day to create time awareness.
(*"We may go outside for 15 minutes."*
"How long did it take to clear the dishes?")

Stand and use arms as hands of the clock.

Money:
— **Use real money.**
— **Give allowance or pay for extra chores.**
— **Play store, restaurant.**
— **Shop for groceries.**
— **Start a business.**

PROBLEM SOLVING

Understand math vocabulary:
less than / more than / larger than / smaller than / same as longer - shorter / before - after / between

Understand signs: $+$, $-$, $=$, *etc.*

Analyze a story problem:
— **Discuss the problem.**
— **Look for and mark clue words.**
— **Write a number sentence after reading the story problem.**
— **Visually represent numerical amounts.**
— **Diagram and discuss problems together.**
— **Encourage your child to use visual clues to solve problems.**
— **Sometimes it help to picture the problem.**

Encourage your child to "think math" throughout the day.

Time

Time is also taught best in the home. For one thing, we use real clocks, not just those printed in the textbook. Use a clock with moveable hands and clear, well spaced numbers. (See box below showing the sequence for teaching time.) Start with the simple and move to the complex.

SEQUENCE FOR TEACHING TIME
Hour
1/2 hour
1/4 hour
5 minute intervals
before and after hour
minutes, seconds

As you teach your child to *tell* time, also help him become *aware* of time. Talk about time in your daily lives. *"I would like for you to take 15 minutes to prepare yourself for school by brushing your hair, brushing your teeth, and straightening your room."* Then set the timer and let him experience 15 exact minutes. The child learns the meaning of segments of time. Or say, *"In 15 minutes we will go outside."* Or, *"How long did it take you to sweep the front porch?"*

Teach longer ranges of time, too. For example, *"How many months until your next birthday?" "How many days will it be before Saturday?"* (Anytime after Labor Day, the retailers will help you countdown to Christmas.)

Money

The last aspect of computation is money. In the home you can give your child many experiences involving real money instead of those little pictures in workbooks used to teach currency.

Play store at home. While you're at it, use real quarters, dimes, and nickels. At our house, when one child was learning about currency, we used real money and played restaurant at lunch time over a period of weeks. The children purchased grilled cheese sandwiches and drinks. They added totals and gave me, the waitress, the correct amount. You better believe I expected a good tip, too!

Take your child to the grocery store. Let him estimate and add the cost of purchases before arriving at the checkout counter. He can comparison shop by looking at unit pricing to see what is the best buy for the money. He can deduct the cents off coupons to see what the total cost is and figure out the amount of sales tax owed for a purchase.

Eventually you turn the corner into true real-life learning. If you give your child an allowance or pay for jobs, he can figure out 10% by tithing, make purchases and figure out change. He can put the money in the bank and add up his totals.

• Twelve-year-old Debra (who likes hands-on learning) has developed a system of money management that works for her. She categorizes budget areas and keeps the money she earns in envelopes. Ten percent of all earnings go into the Lord's envelope. A large portion is set aside for mission trips she hopes to take. (When this envelope bulges, Debra takes it to the bank where she has a savings account for her missions fund.) Another portion is set aside for gifts. And a final portion is set aside for clothing purchases.

• Eight-year-old Beth started a flower business one summer. With her own money, she purchased zinnia seeds and fertilizer. She and her Dad tilled a sunny area and waited for the flowers to grow. By mid-summer, Beth's flower baskets were full and she went door-to-door selling flowers. Profits were good, quite good! How did she know? Beth recorded all expenses and income in a notebook, learning simple bookkeeping in the process.

Of course, many homeschoolers across the nation are learning the use and application of money by working in their parent's home businesses. Teach your children what you're doing and they'll learn more than just how to figure sales tax.

Problem Solving

Actually, we've just talked about several examples of problem-solving in our discussion of computation. But problem-solving also includes those word problems most of us dreaded. Remember? —

"Both families are going to Grandma's for Thanksgiving. If the train is traveling at 90 mph, the car is traveling at 45 mph, and they must both go 300 kilometers, when will the turkey be done?"

(Hold on math buffs... wait 'til *later* to solve that one.)

In order to be able to deal with a written problem, a child must be able to read and understand it. If your child can't read and understand a particular problem, don't penalize him. Read it aloud, walk him through it.

Word problems are not a reading test! Read them *with* the child if you have to. Notice I didn't say read the problems *to* the child, I said read the problems *with* the child. This means you just walk through the problems with the child phrase by phrase for understanding. Have the child read a section to you, interpret it, read a section to you, interpret it.

Rev. 92

Clue your child in to key words. ("How much more" is a key phrase.) Math has its own unique vocabulary — longer, shorter, before, after, between, larger than, smaller than, same as. Even with fluent readers, it's a good idea to look at the problems your child will be doing on a given day and key him into the math vocabulary ahead of time to avoid frustration. Just as you introduce new vocabulary words before a passage is read, you introduce math vocabulary before it is used if your child needs it.

Your child needs to know how to analyze a story problem. Your discussion together is so important, but sometimes you may want to soften the ground first. If reading ability isn't the issue, have a child who finds word problems difficult go off alone to read one problem. This gives him thinking time without you breathing down his neck. It takes the pressure off and gives him a head start.

He should analyze the parts of the problem and write out the information given in the problem. Write an analysis of the story problem. Let's do a simple one.

Sara has 11 matchbox cars.
She gives 6 blue ones to her brother.
How many matchbox cars are left?

First, you teach him to write the information given —

ll = number of cars
6 = number of cars given away.
How many cars are left?

The key word in the question is "*left.*" That word signals the problem is a subtraction problem. If you have your child analyze problems in writing, it will force him to think through them. If you need to, represent the parts of the problems with manipulatives such as beads, raisins, matchbox cars, etc. (Older children should be told to actually visualize the problem, not just look at isolated numbers and guess what to do with them.) Ever met someone with a knack for solving real-life problems? Our goal is to help our youngsters understand *why* so deeply that they develop a feel for attacking problems.

While in the car, make up word problems that prod your child to apply math to daily life. It will be a mental effort for you, but it will pay dividends. (On second thought, maybe you'd better make up the problems *before* you start driving.)

Final thoughts on teaching math

When teaching math, never just tell the right answer. If your child doesn't know how to work a problem, ask questions rather than just telling how to work a problem. Always go through the steps it takes to explain the *why* of the right answer. And impress upon your child that knowing *why* is even more important than knowing the right answer.

Remember — if math is "learned" without meaning, this will cause frustration later. Don't let your child think math can be learned in a cookbook fashion. (*"Tell me the steps, I'll follow them by rote, but don't ask me to explain why something works."*) Higher levels of thinking require a foundation of understanding.

Frequent word problems are best. It's better to do one or two each day, than 10 on a page one day and none the next 5 days in a row. Again, understanding the procedure is more important than getting a "right" answer. So take your time. The object is not to rush through a book. Stop when either of you tire out.

Do give your child mental math drills. *"5 times 4 plus 3 plus 2 divided by 5 equals what?"* Just don't drill facts until you are sure the child understands.

Do you see why this section began with a discussion on problem-solving? What are we trying to accomplish? We're trying to raise children who can use what they learn to solve real-life problems, and creatively use all the knowledge at their disposal.

DAILY MATH HABITS

Short daily cumulative review.

Manipulatives to introduce a new concept.

Lesson from structured curriculum.

Real life problem solving.

Brain teasers, puzzles, tricks.

Mental math drill.

Stress care in daily math work.
Careless mistakes carry over into daily life math and standardized tests.

Notes:

Notes:

Rev. 92011

Appendix A
Choosing Curriculum

Want to be ready for the Spring bookfairs? Not only will exhibitors offer "how-to" workshops, but also red-hot "today only!" specials on some materials. *And* you'll have a chance to save on shipping charges. When the pressure's on, will you know how to choose intelligently? Or, will all those selections baffle and confuse you, like a child entering a department store for the first time?

It makes sense to prepare ahead before shopping for a year's resources. Start by asking, *"What do I hope to accomplish with my children next year?"* Then set a budget and make a basic shopping list. Both will help you avoid impulse decisions.

Still feel like you need more help? Okay, let's look at what you need to know to equip your family for a successful school year.

Set a Budget

Before you shop for curriculum, set a budget. To select the best materials you can afford, make your homeschool supplies a priority. New homeschooling parents often ask, *"How much do I have to spend?"* My answer to this is, *"Don't skimp if you can help it."*

If money's short, think of fund raising ideas. Have a yard sale, volunteer to clean someone's house, mow a lawn. Do whatever you can to establish a reasonable money supply for your children's education. Then assess where your money is spent. Are you subscribing to expensive correspondence courses that charge a premium for supervision? That cash might be better spent on major purchases, like a classroom microscope (not a toy) or a manipulative math kit.

Review Annual Goals

If you prayerfully set and write annual goals for your children, the natural next step is to choose curriculum which reflects those goals. Is character training a priority this year? Then look for materials focused on Godly character traits.

Is this the year you'll attempt to teach beginning reading? Then *your* priority would be a good phonics program. (By the way, price is not always an indicator of what is good. *"Am I comfortable using this?"* is a better indicator.)

Or perhaps a goal for your children this year is to sharpen reasoning skills. Then choose materials that aren't geared towards short, quick answers, but which emphasize projects and discovery. Or for the young child, you may feel this is the year to build a foundation of experience (in science, for example). Choose child-centered resources which give you ideas for activities, rather than just reading material.

Before you shop, involve your children in decision-making. Ask them about their interests. Let them help choose topics for the whole family to study. Many families are successfully choosing limited subject areas, digging deeply, and becoming experts in specific areas (i.e., unit studies).

For example, as one fourth grader studied the state of Vermont this year, she became an expert on maple sugar production. She read several books on the topic, then gave an oral presentation that included visuals, notecards, etc. She also researched and tested products and recipes. This took a week, but reading, written and oral language, math experience, and other skill areas were developed — not to mention all she learned about Vermont.

A curriculum is merely a tool you use to accomplish your objectives. It will never replace the teacher (you), or the child. Remain goal-oriented throughout the school year, rather than paper production-oriented. Goal-oriented teachers master the curriculum. Paper production-oriented teachers are mastered by their curriculum.

Know the Basic Areas of Study

What are the basic areas of study to keep in mind as you plan your curriculum choices? To simplify matters, I tell parents to focus on two major areas: the *3-R's* (reading, writing, arithmetic), plus *units of study*.

Cover the 3-R's well, with age/ability appropriate materials. Choose one core curriculum for beginning reading instruction (it's counterproductive to have a "reading" textbook for older children), another for math instruction. Choose materials that will teach *you* to teach your child to write compositions. Select grammar workbooks only if this is the "season" for it.

Phonics, grammar, and math require sequential teaching, building precept upon precept. For example, in phonics the child first learns the letter sounds, moves to blends, then to words. Add life to your core curriculum, supplement with kits and games — just don't mistake them for a full program. (Some have mistakenly thought a math kit was a total curriculum when it was never intended as such.)

Once you've taken care of the 3-R's, focus on your unit study needs. (See Section Three, **Pulling It All Together**.) Will this be the year your family studies colonial history? Will you spend a semester covering life science topics? You be the judge!

Want to save hours of planning and learn from others without reinventing the wheel? While shopping, take a look at prepared unit study materials designed specifically for homeschoolers.

Know the Categories of Curriculum

Curriculum can be categorized in four basic ways. First, there are *highly structured programs*. These include video classroom tapes and workbooks, correspondence schools, and worktext programs. Highly structured programs may help the first year teacher or one who needs discipline and guidelines, but there are drawbacks.

Our first semester of home school was spent in a highly structured program. My oldest child and I learned to schedule and focus on school, rather than all the distractions I had been used to before (telephone calls, women's groups, outside interests). After one semester though, I felt like a "noose" was around my neck. My child was definitely tired of workbook pages, too...

Discovery! *Use workbooks with discretion!*

Workbooks are useful for teaching subjects like grammar or typing. They're also effective for teaching basics, like math or phonics, but children who spend the better part of each day in them will soon grow weary, and the time you save in preparation will be wasted trying to motivate your child.

You may find yourself gravitating towards highly structured programs out of insecurity, when in fact a little teacher training is all you need. If so, attend "How to" workshops and study teacher help books in the summer. (There's a resource list at the end of this appendix.)

The second curriculum category is *moderately structured*. This includes typical textbooks and teacher's manuals. Moderately structured materials have daily lessons, but you decide how the lessons are used and answer only to yourself. Again, they may especially help you with the basics.

Most textbooks are written for a room full of students so you must modify the lessons to suit your tutorial teaching style. By now, you realize homeschool is *not* a classroom placed in your living room. It's unique! When selecting textbooks, ask yourself whether the lessons will be difficult to adapt to the home setting.

Be especially cautious when you review typical history or science texts. For elementary grade youngsters, avoid "survey" style textbooks. Young children benefit more from in-depth experiences. (For example, science lessons should emphasize doing and discovering, rather than reading about science.) Later, in high school, they will be better able to see the "big picture."

The third category of curriculum is unique to the home schooling movement. These are *unit studies materials* designed to integrate several subject areas under one topic. For example, when you study the United States, you might make salt dough maps (geography/art), learn about Norman Rockwell's art (art appreciation), read aloud **Walk Across America**, (literature/social studies), dress as cowboys and dramatize a rodeo (drama), or take a walking tour of your city (social studies/field trip).

Don't pay a premium to buy a lot of paper. Look for unit study materials that help *you* help your children *discover* the answers. In fact, watch out for materials that only tell the information or that rely exclusively on paper and pencil assignments (reading books, writing reports, drawing maps, etc.)

Also, don't let a program box youngsters into topics that bore them. For example, when studying U.S. industry, my seventh grader was assigned a research paper on any topic related to industry. She wasn't interested in factories, business giants, or Wall Street. What she really wanted to learn about was oceanography, particularly plant life. After some discussion, we realized she could research a new and growing industry — aquaculture. Interest soared and she became an "expert" in seaweed.

The last curriculum category is *supplementary kits or games*. They add sparkle to your basic choices. For example, math games supplement traditional textbooks. Science kits or experiment books are also great extras. Save room in your budget for some sparkle.

Have Fun Learning Together
You're part of it! — a movement across our nation developing a unique style of education. While classroom teachers are understandably restricted in their choices (by a valid need for "crowd control"), you can accomplish the basics in less time, and allow for more time spent discovering, experiencing, and reasoning together. Have fun learning together as a family!

Ready... Set... Go!
Now that you know the basics of "curriculum assessment" you can wade through the book tables with confidence. Enjoy yourself. Remember — You're the expert. You know what's best for you and your family.

RESOURCES

Listed below are recommended teacher helps and materials related to reading, written language, and math. This list is by no means complete, but it will help get you started. Check out these items at the next homeschool book fair or through your local homeschool book distributor...

Teacher Helps

You Can Teach Your Child Successfully
Ruth Beechick, Education Services.

The Three R's
Ruth Beechick, Education Services.

How to Home School,
A Practical Approach
Gayle Graham

How to Create Your Own Unit Study
Valerie Bendt

The Unit Study Idea Book
Valerie Bendt

Success with Unit Studies
Valerie Bendt

How to Help Children Who Have Difficulty Learning
Katherine S. Koonce

How to Help Children Who Have Difficulty Paying Attention
Katherine S. Koonce

The Parenting Tool Kit
Dr. Dale Simpson

We Home School
Debbie Strayer

Math

Math Sense Building Blocks Program
Katherine S. Koonce
Susan S. Simpson

100 Sheep (Skip Counting Tape & Booklet)
Roger Nichols

3 - Way Math Cards

Grocery Cart Math
Jaye Hansen

Reading

The Common Sense Reading Program
Debbie Strayer
Susan Simpson
(Grade 1 handwriting, reading aloud, phonics)

Reading Skills Discovery Series

Bookshelf Collections

For the Love of Reading
Valerie Bendt

The Frances Study Guide
Valerie Bendt

Creating Books with Children
Valerie Bendt

Written Language:

**Learning Language Arts
Through Literature**
Debbie Strayer
Susan Simpson
Diane Welch
(integrated language arts)

**The Great Editing Adventure
Series**
Yuriko Nichols

Great Explorations in Editing
Yuriko Nichols

Wordsmith Apprentice
Janie Cheaney

Wordsmith
Janie Cheaney

Wordsmith Craftsman
Janie Cheaney

How to Teach Any Child to Spell
Gayle Graham

Tricks of the Trade
Gayle Graham

Appendix B
Understanding
Standardized Testing

Most parent educators love teaching. Merrily they roll along, setting educational goals, implementing a rich learning program throughout the year. Why then, do these same parents who have worked so hard the entire school year freeze with fear when standardized tests are mentioned?

The answer? *Lack of understanding!*

Most parent educators did not take "EDUCATIONAL RESEARCH-501" or "TESTS AND MEASUREMENTS-502" in college. The language of testing is foreign to them. *"Who said percentile doesn't mean percent correct?"* you say. *"It meant percent correct when I was in school."* Or, *"What if there's a concept I haven't taught on the test? Won't that be unfair to my child? The tests are secular, aren't they? Doesn't that mean they're unfairly biased against my child who's in a Christian environment?"*

Let's look together at answers to questions you frequently ask about standardized tests. If you understand what makes them unique — along with a few "how-to's"— you'll be as wise about standardized testing as you are about teaching! Then maybe those standardized tests will be *useful* to you.

What is standardized testing, anyway?

> STANDARDIZED TEST: A TEST GIVEN UNDER A STANDARD OF CONDITIONS, WITH CAREFULLY CHOSEN TEST ITEMS, WHICH REPORT SCORES AS PERCENTILES OR GRADE OR AGE EQUIVALENTS.

The teacher-made history tests you and I took in school were measures of the information covered. Standardized test questions are much more carefully constructed. They are designed to measure specific school-related skills.

After much study of curriculums and children, test makers select questions which reflect whether specific school objectives have been met. For example, a few selected spelling words may be on one standardized test. These words were chosen because they tell us whether or not a child has attained a certain spelling level.

Testmakers know a child of a particular grade level can usually spell certain words. If your child demonstrates he can spell those words, he attains that grade equivalent on that particular test.

After they study various curriculums, testmakers run several sample tests before deciding exactly which test items to include. The fact that they include an item you have not covered does not mean you have failed your child. Tests are designed to sample many, varied curriculums — you are not expected to have covered all items on a standardized test. *No standardized test covers an entire curriculum of a particular school; neither does any one school's curriculum cover all the items on a standardized test!*

Standardized achievement tests are not only made of carefully constructed questions, they are meant to always be given under the same conditions — using precise directions and time limits. Naturally, if the directions or time limits are changed, your child's scores won't be accurate.

How will the test be scored?

After your child takes the test, his scores are compared to the original group of students of the same grade or age who first took the test when the averages (*norms*) were determined (called the *norming sample*). *Norm-referenced* test scores are simply scores that compare your child to that specific group. Your child is not being compared to children other than those in the norm group.

Scores are reported as a percentile rank, or grade or age equivalents. Percentile scores show where the student ranks in relation to the children in the norming sample. A percentile of 68 means your child did as well or better than 68% of those in the sample who were his same age/grade. It does not mean he got 68% correct on the test!

Beware! It's very easy to misinterpret grade equivalent scores! If your second grade daughter receives a 6.3 grade equivalent on a standardized test, it just means on that test she performed as well as the average student in the third month of the sixth grade. Obviously, your second grader has not yet learned all the things she needs to know in grades three through six. What it does mean is that your daughter mastered her second grade material very well. In fact, she probably didn't miss much at all. She may have even reasoned out how to do a few third or fourth grade level problems. On the other hand, the average sixth grader would even miss some second grade items on the test.

Should my child take a group test or an individual test?

Some nationally standardized tests such as the IOWA TESTS OF BASIC SKILLS or the CALIFORNIA ACHIEVEMENT TEST are designed for

Rev. 920

large groups. These tests are simple to administer and relatively low in cost. But are they the best option for homeschool children? You decide!

Individual tests, which are given to one pupil at a time, allow the examiner to gain insight into the child's reasoning and behavior while taking the test. Often individual tests don't have rigid time limits but, instead, the child can take as much time as he needs to answer questions. This may be an important factor in your decision of whether to use a group or individual test. Also, individual tests don't require a separate answer sheet since the examiner is responsible for recording answers. In most cases however, an individual test requires a specially trained examiner for administration. Contact your local home school support group to get names of trusted individual test examiners in your area.

Why do I need a test?
"I know what my child has learned! — I work with him every day!"

Certainly, testing for no reason is purposeless. One reason many home educators use tests is that their state law requires it. You may only be interested in attaining certain percentile scores in order to satisfy the law. Others of you may test because you desire reassurance and an outsider's opinion is valuable to you!

Other valid reasons for testing exist:
- You want to know whether your educational goals have been met. You covered a basic third grade math curriculum this year. How does your third grader compare to other third graders? A grade equivalent or percentile will satisfy you!

- You want to find learning gaps, if any exist, and design appropriate remediation, if necessary.

- You want to use test results to plan for an even better school year next year!

Whether you test for any or all of these reasons, remember that you alone, are the single best judge of what your child has learned! As the teacher, you observed, coached, and ministered each day. You know whether Mike learned his long vowels! Any test will only support your findings, as the teacher.

How do I choose a test?
Evaluate your test choice by asking three questions:

1. *Will this test give me the information I need?*
For a test to be useful to you, it must have content validity. That means it should mirror the curriculum you intended to cover. (By the way, standardized test items are generally not factual.

If your child can read and understand a subject, he can do well on the test about that subject.) Assuming the test covers what you think is *valid content* (*and* assuming that your child didn't just have trouble with test-taking mechanics) low scores tell you one of two things: Either your child didn't remember what he was taught or he wasn't taught what you wanted him to learn.

Low scores may tell you to re-evaluate your curriculum, teaching approach, the learning environment, possible distractions, etc. Maybe your child just needs to take it a bit slower. But never make a judgement on the basis of one test. If your child gets a low score, have another evaluation done by a trained teacher or take a different test.

2. *Does this test make the best use of our time and resources?*
Generally, tests designed for large groups, though inexpensive, take as much as two hours per day over a school week. Is this an appropriate use of your time? If all you want are general scores, an individual survey test may be quicker to administer. Then again, you may have to hire a trained examiner for an individual test and *that* costs you more money.

3. *Is this particular testing situation best for my child?*
How can you tell? Test formats vary. Group tests are usually timed and frequently require answer sheets with those infuriating little dots. While some children have no difficulty transferring answers from a test booklet to an answer sheet or working within time limits, *others do*. Some of you may want your child to have this experience. Others of you may feel this format would prohibit a fair assessment of your child as he may fail "test-taking" rather than the actual test content. In your case, you may want an individual assessment in which the examiner is responsible for recording answers and tests are untimed.

How do I choose an examiner?
Most of you have three basic choices in selecting an examiner: *the state, yourself* (or a homeschool friend), or *a private examiner.*

In many states, standardized testing is offered with the public school group. Group standardized tests such as the Iowa Tests of Basic Skills or SRA (Science Research Associates) may be used. Consider whether going into a strange environment in a large group will provide an unfair testing situation. You may or may not desire this experience for your child.

You may also give the test yourself, or ask a teacher friend to give it. Group standardized tests are easy to administer as long as directions are followed explicitly; however, scoring services will be needed. Contact your state home school organization to see whether they supply standardized tests.

Another resource for tests is Bob Jones University Press. They will send you the IOWA TESTS OF BASIC SKILLS. A person other than yourself must give the test, which is then returned to BJU for scoring. Norm referenced scores are provided on this test.

Hewitt Research Foundation offers PASS (PERSONALIZED ACHIEVEMENT SUMMARY SYSTEM) which is a norm referenced achievement survey that can be given by the parents in the home. Hewitt's testing service is available even to those who are not enrolled in the Hewitt correspondence program, but check to see whether the PASS test is acceptable in your state.

How do I Prepare my Child for Test Taking?

CRAMMING: TRYING TO STUDY FOR A SEMESTER'S WORTH OF BIOLOGY IN THREE HOURS THE NIGHT BEFORE THE EXAM.

Cramming produces stress. Stress produces test anxiety, which is counter-productive. You can teach your child uncomplicated test-taking strategies. (For example, it is more harmful to skip than to take a guess, especially on multiple-choice tests.) Your best role is that of encourager and facilitator. Provide a tranquil, peaceful environment to a well-rested, well-fed child on test day!

How do I Use Test Scores?

You've spent time and money on this test. Shouldn't you have useful information for your investment? Do you just want percentile scores to compare your child to a national sample? Or do you want more?

Maybe you want a test to tell you what your child can do, and not just how he compares to others! Group standardized tests are beginning to include criterion referenced components which break down general scores into subtest scores, providing you with a clearer picture of your child's strengths and weaknesses. Naturally, you will expect an individual test to give you more than general scores because the examiner can record observations and analyze types of questions that were missed, enabling you to better plan for next year.

What you already know about your child is the best evaluation of all! Combine your knowledge with test results to see the whole picture of your child's achievement!

How can I lobby for fair testing of homeschool children?

Now that you're a wise test consumer, it only follows that you should have input into the development of not only the tests themselves, but of laws pertaining to the testing of your children!

As intelligent test consumers, we can affect the development and use of tests by understanding three facets of testing. An acronym to recall these is LAB — which stands for *Limitations*, *Appropriateness*, and *Bias*.

LIMITATIONS — We shouldn't allow school systems to make sweeping judgments about *any* child based on isolated test scores. Tests, as you know, tell only part of a child's school achievement story. These should be coupled with records and observations to make sound decisions regarding placement, etc. His teacher's impressions are just as valid as test results!

For the record, save work samples in your child's 3-ring binder. Looking back through these will remind you of all you learned together. And of course, not everything your child learns can be measured with a test. For example, the ability to remain with a difficult task until finished is not measurable on a test; but it *is* a vital character trait that could be noted in an anecdotal record. At the end of the year, slip those comments into your child's binder.

APPROPRIATENESS— A youngster who has trouble keeping his place on a line might fail on a group standardized test which requires transferring answers to a separate answer sheet. Similarly, children who are having difficulty reading should not be given tests which require much individual reading of directions.

BIAS — If a home-educated child is asked to take a group test in an unfamiliar school setting with a large group of children, doesn't this present an unfair testing situation? Physical and psychological factors are important to the one being tested. *Test makers recommend that tests be given where the child is schooled.*

What about familiarity with test format? Of course, a teacher shouldn't show particular test items in advance to a child, as no one in the norm sample to which he will be compared saw the test items in advance. But, schoolteachers legitimately give a sample test the day before the actual test to familiarize children with test format. As homeschool educators, we should do that for *our* children. Ask the examiner for copies of sample tests to use in advance of the testing day.

Rarely, you may discover test items which reflect a secular or anti-Christian underlying philosophy. If you do discover inappropriate test items, write to the test publishers explaining your differences! Test publishers, who want to sell tests, will respond to public outcry. While you're writing, express the particular needs of home educators. You need tests that you as the parent/educator can buy and give, as well as tests which reflect your curriculum objectives without anti-Christian bias.

Rev. 92

Meanwhile, tell them of your desire to see home educated children included in the next norming sample so that you will be comparing your child to similar children.

Understanding limitations, appropriateness, and bias in testing can help you, as parent/educators, obtain better tests, as well as testing situations, for your children.

Addresses of Test Publishers

California Achievement Tests
CTB McGraw Hill
Del Monte Research Park
Monterey, CA. 93940

Iowa Tests of Basic Skills
Riverside Publishing Co.
P. O. Box 1970
Iowa City, Iowa 52244

Metropolitan Achievement Tests
The Psychological Corporation
757 3rd Avenue
New York, New York 10017

SRA Achievement Series
Science Research Associates, Inc.
155 N. Wacker Dr.
Chicago, Illinois 60606

Stanford Achievement Tests
The Psychological Corporation
757 3rd Avenue
New York, New York 10017

Scholastic Achievement Test (SAT)
Scholastic Testing Service, Inc.
480 Meyer Rd.
Bensenville, Illinois 60106

PASS
Hewitt Research Foundation
PO Box 9
Washougal, WA 98671

Appendix C
Reproducible Forms

On the next several pages are blank forms for your homeschool records. Feel free to reproduce these for your personal use only.

Rev. 920114

HOUSEHOLD CHORES — WEEK AT A GLANCE

Routines reduce stress.
"What do I need to do each day in order to maintain my acceptable standard of cleanliness?"
Break larger chores into smaller chunks (ex. instead of 'dusting entire house', dust 2 rooms per day.
Or instead of having one child do the bathroom, have one do the toilet and floor,
another the shower, and another the sink and mirror.)

Chores:	Daily:
Monday:	
Tuesday:	
Wednesday:	
Thursday:	*Material Distractors to eliminate*
Friday:	*Time Distractors to eliminate*
Saturday:	*Monitor the use of your time... Are you spending it as you desire?*

Curriculum Scope (K-8) for:				
Year	Reading	Written Language	Math	Units

Curriculum Scope (9-12) for:

Literature	Foreign Language	Language	Math	Science	Social Studies	Other

Mom's Week at a Glance

	Monday	Tuesday	Wednesday	Thursday	Friday
6:00					
6:30					
7:00					
7:30					
8:00					
8:30					
9:00					
9:30					
10:00					
10:30					
11:00					
11:30					
NOON					
12:30					
1:00					
1.30					
2:00					
2:30					
3:00					
Late Aft.					
Dinner					
After Dinner					

COORDINATING A NUMBER OF CHILDREN — MASTER PLAN AT A GLANCE

Name:				
8:30				
9:00				
9:30				
10:00				
10:30				
11:00				
11:30				
12:00				
12:30				
1:00				
2:00				
After Dinner				

Note: This is a rotating daily schedule for large families. Use four days per week only.
One day can be hands-on, project day!

ASSIGNMENTS — WEEK AT A GLANCE

Name_____ Week of _____

Subject	Monday	Tuesday	Wednesday	Thursday	Friday
Mom's Notes:					

Unit Plans — Week at a Glance

Unit Topic:_____ **Week #** _____

Reading, Simple Activity

Day 1

Day 2

Day 3

Day 4

Hands-on Day!

Trips?

Supply List

Comments

Sit down and do a whole unit of these at one time. (Use pencil.)
On four days, plan to read and do simple activities. Save one day for experiments, projects, etc.

PROGRAM OF STUDY

Student: _____   *Year:* _____

Reading

Writing

Math

Unit Studies

Registry of Great Reading
by_____

Title	Author	by my hand.. ..on this date

Yearly Goals

Proverbs 8:34 "Blessed is the man who listens to me, watching daily at my gates, waiting at the posts of my door."

Relationship with God		Husband/Wife Relationship
Daily Living	Ministry / Service	

Child	Academic	Spiritual	Physical	Practical

Yearly goals keep us focused. What's really important? Are my priorities balanced?

Monthly Goals

Sept.	Dec.	Mar.	June
Oct.	Jan.	Apr.	July
Nov.	Feb.	May	Aug.

- Write goals / units you will work on each month before planning for the week or day. Use pencil!

- Keep your goals in mind when planning life's daily details.

Checkpoint: Am I willing to give up all my personal expectations and allow God, through a lifetime, to replace my goals with His goals?